Theory

Theory

Norman
Yeung

Playwrights Canada Press
Toronto

For professional or amateur production rights, please contact:
Playwrights Guild of Canada
St. Matthew's Clubhouse, 450 Broadview Ave., Toronto, ON M4K 2N1
416.703.0201

LIBRARY AND ARCHIVES CANADA CATALOGUING IN PUBLICATION
Title: Theory / Norman Yeung.
Names: Yeung, Norman, author.
Description: A play.
Identifiers: Canadiana (print) 20200386832 | Canadiana (ebook) 20200386859 | ISBN 9780369101617 (softcover) | ISBN 9780369101624 (PDF) | ISBN 9780369101631 (HTML) | ISBN 9780369101648 (Kindle)
Classification: LCC PS8647.E96 T54 2020 | DDC C812/.6—dc23

Playwrights Canada Press operates on Mississaugas of the Credit, Wendat, Anishinaabe, Métis, and Haudenosaunee land. It always was and always will be Indigenous land.

We acknowledge the financial support of the Canada Council for the Arts—which last year invested $153 million to bring the arts to Canadians throughout the country—the Ontario Arts Council (OAC), Ontario Creates, and the Government of Canada for our publishing activities.

Canada Council for the Arts | Conseil des arts du Canada

ONTARIO ARTS COUNCIL
CONSEIL DES ARTS DE L'ONTARIO
an Ontario government agency
un organisme du gouvernement de l'Ontario

Canada

ONTARIO CREATES | ONTARIO CRÉATIF

I dedicate my first book to my family.

Class Is in Session

April Sizemore-Barber

Save for a few detours into virtual and domestic space, the majority of *Theory*'s action occurs beneath the fluorescent lights of a college lecture hall. For those of us who teach, this bland backdrop serves as an electric and unpredictable staging space: part creative crucible, part political powder keg. As one of the few realms where people from vastly different backgrounds enter into discussion, the classroom—at least, in theory—contains unlimited democratic potential. Yet, as Norman Yeung's taut technothriller powerfully demonstrates, questions of identity, power, and representation are rarely theoretical. Debates that begin as dispassionate inquiry in classrooms can spiral out into public spaces and they come with unforeseen consequences.

Our protagonist, Isabelle, is a young film professor who strongly believes that the classroom should be a place for multiple viewpoints, where no subject is out of bounds and academic hierarchies are made to be dismantled. On the first day of the semester, she dramatically enacts this philosophy, ripping up the mandated Film Theory syllabus and inviting her students to push back against canons and take charge of their education. Overriding student trepidation, she encourages them to post anonymously on the course's online message board. The anonymity, she explains, will allow them to have difficult, honest conversations without judgment or fear of surveillance.

Yet the Internet has proven to be a double-edged sword. Where Isabelle idealistically views technology as a catalyst for the free circulation of ideas, her digital-native students experience it as an unpredictable den of trolls. Isabelle's film classes, which encourage undergraduates to critically engage with controversial films such as *The Birth of a Nation* and *Triumph of the Will*, do not sit well with her multicultural student body. To them, being asked to view films notorious for serving as recruitment tools for the Ku Klux Klan and Nazi Germany, whatever their importance to film history, is itself a form of violence. These images, they argue, cannot be dissociated from their contemporary circulation on social media by newly emboldened neo-fascists and white supremacists. Where Isabelle seeks to offer her students autonomy, they crave her guidance rather than provocation. The unmoderated message board devolves into a microcosm of the larger cultural climate, fuelled by personal attacks, bigoted vitriol, and explicit imagery. When an anonymous student with an axe to grind weaponizes the board to undermine Isabelle in the classroom and, disturbingly, encroach upon her personal life, she is forced to reconsider her methods. By this point, however, it may be too late. Pandora's (in) Box has been opened.

As a gender studies professor teaching in the same hair-trigger, polarized climate of the play, I had a visceral response upon first reading the script. Indeed, I immediately sent a flurry of texts to director Victoria Murray Baatin, who had asked me to dramaturge the US premiere: "This is literally my worst nightmare," "I love it!" and "Let's do it!" I saw my own classroom experiences reflected back to me in Isabelle's struggle. Wanting to open young minds and encourage critical thought, we professors frequently find ourselves on the front lines of a culture war that we have not been prepared to fight. Many of us, particularly my colleagues shunted to adjunct contracts that pay little and provide no health insurance, exist in positions of sustained precarity, dependent on notoriously fickle student evaluations and university largesse for our continued employment. And we all have our war stories—mine involve a student turning informant for a right-wing publication that branded me a Cultural Marxist (the horror!), leading to an alarming influx of hate mail from readers. We still believe in those "Aha!" moments in the classroom, when a student feels heard or comes into their own voice. Yet we're also aware of the very real risks involved, some of which are dramatized in this play.

Theory addresses perennial themes through the prism of our uniquely troubled times. In the years since it was written and first performed, its questions have only become more relevant and its stakes more clearly urgent. As so much of life has been forced online by the COVID-19 pandemic, once-discrete spaces of "work," "home," and "school" have begun to blend and blur into a virtual morass. #CancelCulture and trigger warnings are now part of everyday parlance and mistrust between different communities is stoked by high anxiety. Yeung's script digs into this conundrum, cutting through the knee-jerk cacophony of social media and using the dialogical space of the theatre to stage an extended meditation on technology, community, and representation. While *Theory* may not give us all the answers, like the best sort of Socratic seminar, it poses all the right questions.

April Sizemore-Barber is Assistant Professor of the Practice, Women's and Gender Studies, at Georgetown University. Her research is located at the intersection of performance, queer, and Africana studies, and has been published in Theatre Journal, Theatre Topics, *and Safundi: The Journal of South African and American Studies. She has recently published her first book,* Prismatic Performances: Queer South Africa and the Fragmentation of the Rainbow Nation *(University of Michigan Press, 2020), which traces the intersections of performance, South African queer identity, and concepts of post-apartheid citizenship. She served as dramaturge for* Theory's *US premiere at DC's Mosaic Theater in 2019.*

Playwright's Notes

That *Theory* has gained urgency and relevance since I wrote the first draft in 2009 is uncanny. Over a decade of innumerable workshops, readings, and productions, my challenge was to revise the script while navigating a socio-political-cultural environment that was changing faster than our climate; an environment moving so fast that when I started writing this play freedom of speech was a liberal value, and somewhere along the way it became conservative.

The protagonist, Isabelle, grew from a champion of free speech, to free thought, to giving voice to the voiceless. Her progressiveness became more complex as political positions became more complicated and liberals increasingly fought amongst themselves. Her complexity is very human, like my friend who advocates for freedom of speech as much as she does for Bernie Sanders and Alexandria Ocasio-Cortez. As Isabelle and *Theory* were developing in lockstep with shifting progressive values, I was reassessing how I write.

Writing whatever a writer wants, especially about experiences not their own, includes the risk of being irresponsible. Writers should be allowed to use their imagination but should also heed boundaries to what story they tell; it's incumbent upon the writer to engage people whose communities are represented in the work as part of the process of writing. My journey with crafting *Theory* is reflected in the evolution of Isabelle's wife, Lee.

Lee was originally a white man. He was Isabelle's boyfriend and played a smaller role in terms of plot and theme. Many of the dynamics and tensions within intersectionality were absent in this early script. In 2013, my dramaturge, the playwright Shirley Barrie, suggested Isabelle not merely profess progressiveness, but live a progressive life. "What if she were married to a woman?" I said yes. As my impulse is to always choose a colourful cast and because explosive debates over the film *The Birth of a Nation* are crucial to the story, the choice was laid bare before me: Lee would be a Black woman, and *Theory* would become a new play.

At one workshop in 2018, Audrey Dwyer, who was playing Lee, had concerns that if her character used to be an activist for social justice, how could she be so tolerant of Isabelle's missteps? She generously offered to go through the script, page by page, with me and director Esther Jun, to locate moments where Lee's reactions—or lack thereof—were not congruent with Isabelle's aggressions, micro and macro. By sharing her personal experience and perspective, Audrey was doing so much more than providing accuracy and believability to this relationship—she was giving Lee a soul, and now the heart of the story is Lee awakening her partner. And I was reawakened to the value of listening to an artist I can trust.

Since the SummerWorks production in 2010, I'd trusted Sascha Cole with informing how I wrote Isabelle. She played the lead role multiple times, right up until 2018, and even though Isabelle's ethics were constantly evolving, Sascha's curiosity and commitment to exploring the character were unwavering. What she brought to rehearsals would find its way into the script; she had such inventiveness and a grasp on the character that I would write with Sascha's voice in my head. And yes, she played Isabelle when Lee was a dude.

I also trust Esther profoundly. If I was the play's engine, she was the engineer. Through workshops to recordings to productions, she often understood the play better than I did. Her warmth and patience made it easy for me to seek her counsel and admit ignorance, especially in matters involving two female lead characters. Esther was my creative confidante who was instrumental in having this play professionally premiere at Tarragon Theatre in October 2018.

After *Theory*'s first preview, I was sitting in the house with Tarragon's artistic director Richard Rose and literary manager Joanna Falck. Things felt grim as I was sagely advised to cut ten pages. "Excuse me," a polite voice chimed in through the sober notes session. "My name's

Victoria Murray Baatin. I'm here from Mosaic Theater in Washington, DC." Victoria had praise and enthusiasm for what *Theory* was saying and saw the vision despite a clunky preview. She requested the script and wanted to stay in touch. I turned to Richard and Joanna, and etched on my redemptive smile were the words, "I guess my play doesn't suck?" I still had to cut ten pages. They were right.

Mosaic Theater Company of DC would produce *Theory*, and I was guided through revisions by Victoria as the director, artistic director Ari Roth, and dramaturge April Sizemore-Barber. Over the years, I've consulted numerous professors so I knew I wasn't off the mark, but now I could work with someone who lent a closer understanding of Isabelle's world—April was Assistant Professor of the Practice, Women's and Gender Studies, at Georgetown University. For this American production in late 2019, was I now off the mark? April noted no egregious errors.

Still, I was anxious about bringing my play to America. There's a lot of filth and bigotry in *Theory*. I've sometimes wondered if I'd gone too far with the students' offensive postings, but then, against better judgment, I read YouTube comments and, yup . . . real life is way worse. Emboldened by free speech, *Theory*'s mysterious student injects racial tension into Isabelle and Lee's home, forcing the couple to confront an issue they'd never had to before: Isabelle's reluctance to silence the student makes her complicit to racism against her wife.

So let's talk about race. I was born in China and immigrated to Canada when I was a baby. I've seen race my entire life. Don't be fooled by our "politeness"—Canada has a sickening racism problem, especially toward our Indigenous and Black populations. America has a different narrative, and given its history, demographics, culture, and media might, racism in America seems especially pronounced, violent, and stark. I was apprehensive about how *Theory* would resonate not just in America, but in DC, where the Black population is the majority and where so many civil rights battles were fought. I don't mind if my work offends people's sensitivities, but if I offend people fundamentally because my work seems irresponsible, reckless, disrespectful . . . then I'm just being an asshole. And if I seem irresponsible regarding race, then that's far more problematic than being an asshole.

Our first preview in DC included many people of colour in the audience. When an act of racism was about to happen on stage, I braced myself and hoped the audience would be patient to see it through, that it had context and served the narrative. One man walked out. Over the next four previews and opening night, with several post-show discussions in between, audience members approached me. They were positive and enthusiastic, some vigorously. Oftentimes they were Black women. At one talkback, without it being the subject at hand, one woman said she believed Lee and Isabelle's marriage.

My self-doubt became more manageable when I reminded myself of the collaborative process of writing this play; *Theory* had found assured guides its entire existence. Victoria handled the material with the flair and confidence that comes from deeply understanding how this play would engage her DC community. She certainly wouldn't allow irresponsible portrayals on her stage. Nor would Andrea Harris Smith, who played Lee in DC. Nor would Audrey, who helped shape Lee to correct my formerly errant writing of the character. I could trust the encouragement and constructive feedback I'd received from LGBTQ+ actors and audience members over the years, whose thoughts helped my revisions. I could have faith in what I learned from collaborating with the directors—every one of them a woman, woman of colour, or man of colour—who provided an experienced voice to this story about two women fighting institutionalized patriarchy and racism. About a character learning from others. That *Theory* remains of the moment after twelve years is a credit to all the people who advised me along the way. All I had to do was listen if I wanted to learn.

Norman Yeung
East Vancouver, January 2021

Theory premiered at Tarragon Theatre in Toronto from October 16 to November 25, 2018, and was produced by Tarragon Theatre with the following cast and creative team:

Isabelle: Sascha Cole
Lee: Audrey Dwyer
Owen: Fabrizio Filippo
Richard: Kyle Orzech
Safina: Asha James
Jorge: Anthony Perpuse
Davinder: Bilal Baig

Director: Esther Jun
Set and Lighting Design: Joseph Pagnan
Projection Design: Cameron Davis
Costume Design: Michelle Bohn
Sound Design: John Gzowski
Fight Director: Jennifer Dzialoszynski
Stage Manager: Robin Munro
Assistant Lighting Design: Jeff Pybus
Assistant Director: Stephanie Williams

Theory had its American premiere at the Atlas Performing Arts Center in Washington, DC, from October 23 to November 17, 2019, and was produced by Mosaic Theater Company of DC with the following cast and creative team:

Isabelle: Musa Gurnis
Lee: Andrea Harris Smith
Owen: Tony K. Nam
Richard: Josh Adams
Safina: Tyasia Velines
Jorge: Camilo Linares
Davinder: Benairen Kane

Director: Victoria Murray Baatin
Set Design: Daniel Ettinger
Lighting Design: Brittany Shemuga
Projection Design: Dylan Uremovich
Costume Design: Danielle Preston
Sound Design: David Lamont Wilson
Properties: Willow Watson
Fight Director: Paul Gallagher
Stage Managers: April E. Carter and Laurel VanLandingham
Assistant Director: Ashara Crutchfield
Dramaturge: April Sizemore-Barber

Theory was presented earlier in developmental productions at Rumble Theatre's Tremors Festival (Vancouver, 2018), Alumnae Theatre Company's FireWorks Festival (Toronto, 2013), and SummerWorks (Toronto, 2010).

The writing of *Theory* was supported by grants from the Canada Council for the Arts, the Ontario Arts Council, and the Toronto Arts Council.

Characters

Isabelle: Thirty. White. Professor of film theory. Struggles with her principles.
Lee: Forty. Black. Tenured professor and novelist. Compromises her values to succeed.
Owen: Forty to fifty. Head of film department. Acknowledges the power students have in campus culture.
Richard: Nineteen. Student. Bright and inquisitive.
Safina: Nineteen. Student. Righteous and vociferous.
Jorge: Nineteen. Student. Critical and shit-disturbing.
Davinder: Nineteen. Student. Altruistic and manipulative.
Camera Operator: Any age, any gender. (The Camera Operator can be played by anyone in the cast except the actor playing Richard.)

Notes

Isabelle and Lee are an interracial, same-sex couple.

Anonymous, generic Students can be played by various groupings of the actors playing Richard, Safina, Jorge, and Davinder. Alternatively, Students' dialogue can be projected instead of spoken.

Images from copyrighted films need not be shown, and may instead be suggested. Original content—images, video, etc.—can be created. *The Birth of a Nation* and *Battleship Potemkin* are in the public domain and can be shown without restriction.

ISABELLE in the lecture hall.

ISABELLE: Thoughts?

Pause.

Enjoy using it. Now let's take a look at the syllabus and— Yes?

RICHARD: Will you be reading it?

ISABELLE: Yes.

JORGE: Will you be using it?

ISABELLE: No.

JORGE: If you're reading it then you're using it.

ISABELLE: Only to offer help, answer questions—

JORGE: That's using it.

ISABELLE: I had the discussion board made for *you*, not me. Let's take a look at the syllabus and— Yes?

RICHARD: Why do we have two?

ISABELLE: I was *just* about to— Yeah?

DAVINDER: So you're the moderator?

ISABELLE: Of the discussion board? Absolutely not.

DAVINDER: Then who is?

ISABELLE: Yourselves.

DAVINDER: So, no one. Like, look at us.

ISABELLE: You all deserve more credit than people give you.

DAVINDER: Have you even looked at a forum?

ISABELLE: Yes. You'll hold each other accountable to your right to speak. And be listened to.

RICHARD: Will you be grading what we say on the board?

ISABELLE: I wouldn't know it's you. You don't have to register your student IDs.

JORGE: No way . . .

ISABELLE: Way. Now everyone take a look at this syllabus. The first one.

JORGE: No way. Everything's recorded on school servers.

ISABELLE: Not if the board was made outside the university.

SAFINA: You can't do that.

ISABELLE shrugs.

ISABELLE: Meh.

JORGE: Dope!

ISABELLE: Yes it is dope. But stay on topic. The board is for discussions about theory. Film criticism, media's role in society . . . The board is not for who's gonna make sandwiches for craft services or other matters from your production course. And no gossip, god please!

DAVINDER: Could you please delete if we do?

ISABELLE: Absolutely not. The board is your responsibility.

SAFINA: That's a lot of responsibility we weren't asking for.

ISABELLE: It's time teachers and students started trusting each other again.

DAVINDER: Yeah no, you can't, like, just do forcible trusting on us.

RICHARD: What if we don't want to use it?

ISABELLE: Why wouldn't you—? Hey. My class will not be a lecture: me to you. *Our* class will be a dialogue and I encourage you all to speak up, which some of you have no problem doing thank you very much. We'll be learning from each other and that means talking to each other. Shutting down someone's thoughts ain't cool in this room. Same with the board, okay? Keep sharing ideas beyond this lecture hall, especially those of you who feel more comfortable speaking online instead of in front of a hundred students. You're included in our community.

DAVINDER: You might wanna be like "um maybe not" on the anonymous part.

ISABELLE: You can use your real name. Up to you. Your identity is yours: your name, your pronoun, your words . . . Don't you feel *empowered?*

Silence.

JORGE: Yeah.

ISABELLE: Okay! Syllabus. The first one. This is the one handed to me by the department. Look at it . . . Buncha dead white dudes . . . We've been shown their images and told their stories for over a hundred years. Now rip it out.

STUDENTS hesitate.

RICHARD: Does it matter that they're dead white dudes if their films are masterpieces?

ISABELLE: Gotta make room for new masterpieces. Rip.

They rip the page out of their binders.

Are you aware that all of you are oppressed by the institution? Obscene tuition and student loans. Rules about how to think. Not being seen or heard. Use your voice to poke holes through the institution, or better yet . . .

She scrunches her paper.

Crush it.

STUDENTS scrunch up their pages. SAFINA hesitates.

You too. C'mon! Ball it up.

SAFINA scrunches.

Now toss it. Chuck it. Hurl it.

STUDENTS toss with rambunctious hooting. SAFINA lobs hers unenthusiastically.

Now look at the second syllabus. Glowing in front of you. This is *our* syllabus. Thoughts?

JORGE: Still some dead white dudes.

ISABELLE: Yes! Some films and directors I'm not *allowed* to omit. The institution considers them mandatory. Let's consider it studying the opposition. But look: I've included Agnès Varda, Maya Deren, Lynne Ramsay, Sofia Coppola, Samira Makhmalbaf, Ava DuVernay . . . Queer cinema, Indigenous and Third Cinema . . . Yes?

RICHARD: Can we post on the board how we feel about your choices?

ISABELLE: Excellent! Great way to use it! . . . Or, you could just . . . tell me now?

SAFINA: You're making us watch a movie called *Baise-moi*?

ISABELLE: Directed by Virginie Despentes and Coralie Trinh Thi, 2000.

SAFINA: We're gonna watch that?

ISABELLE: Only clips. When we get to feminist cinema.

SAFINA: But it means . . . the title . . .

JORGE: What?

SAFINA: It means "fuck me." Sorry.

RICHARD laughs.

ISABELLE: Yes it does.

ISABELLE in her office getting ready to leave. LEE is looking around the space.

LEE: Of course your office would be double the size of mine. And you're a rookie.

ISABELLE: You make double my salary.

LEE: Closer to triple.

ISABELLE pouts.

Awww! Show me some white-woman tears!

ISABELLE feigns cute-crying. They laugh and embrace. Kiss affectionately.

ISABELLE: I've joined your club. Gimme some time, we'll be making equal pay.

LEE: You're tenure *track*. And when you get your raise, it won't be because of time.

ISABELLE: Hey now.

LEE: Merit.

LEE gives her a peck on the cheek.

ISABELLE: 'Kay, let's go home.

ISABELLE opens the door to discover SAFINA standing there, just about to knock.

SAFINA: Sorry! Didn't mean to— Hi, I'm Safina from Theory. I know it's not office hours—

ISABELLE: No no, it's cool. Don't worry about office hours. You're welcome to come right in whenever I'm here. Oh, this is my wife, Lee.

SAFINA: Oh, I . . . Cool!

LEE: Stick to office hours.

Glare from ISABELLE.

ISABELLE: What's up?

SAFINA: I just wanted you to know I won't be coming to certain classes. You're not allowed to show this stuff at a university.

ISABELLE: Have you watched these films before?

SAFINA: I don't have to to know I feel threatened by your choices.

ISABELLE: They're just films.

LEE: Izzy.

ISABELLE: Thanks for telling me how you feel. The best way to get over discomfort is to learn more about what makes you uncomfortable.

SAFINA: Then next class you should ask us what we're uncomfortable watching.

ISABELLE: Here, let's go through the syllabus together and—

SAFINA: That was a waste of paper.

LEE: You pulled your paper stunt.

ISABELLE: I recycled.

SAFINA: It's not just me. I'm speaking for a lot of us.

ISABELLE: Why don't you post about this on the discussion board!

SAFINA: If we all spoke up, would you make changes?

ISABELLE: I spent the entire summer designing this— Is this a political, religious thing?

SAFINA: Okay, that's rude.

LEE: Her syllabus was approved by the department but it's okay if you miss some classes.

SAFINA: Isn't it discrimination to bring up religion?

SAFINA leaves.

ISABELLE: Don't ever do that again.

LEE: You're welcome.

ISABELLE at home. She sits at her computer and sifts through the class discussion board. Someone has posted a video.

ISABELLE: Ooh! New post! . . . *Jungle Fever.*

The video is followed by a quote, big like a headline.

Projection: "The only thing I like integrated is my coffee."

So many comments.

STUDENT: "Whatever, we can marry anyone we want now. This video's irrelevant."

STUDENT: "You sound like a complacent moron who says you don't see race."

ISABELLE AND STUDENT: "Watch Isabelle take this down."

ISABELLE: . . . Keep talking . . .

She continues scrolling through the discussion board.

ISABELLE in the lecture hall. She watches the projection screen, busy searching for a film clip.

SAFINA: Black man dating a white woman . . .

JORGE: *Jungle Fever.*

SAFINA: . . . with that thing about coffee!

JORGE: That's from *Malcolm X.*

DAVINDER: Tell her to take it down.

JORGE: Don't.

RICHARD: Ssshhh!

ISABELLE: What's up, guys?

STUDENTS hush.

. . . So you see how Griffith handled simultaneous action by crosscutting scenes of the African Americans attacking with the Klansmen rescuing—

SAFINA raises her hand.

JORGE: *(to SAFINA)* Come on!

SAFINA: Shouldn't this movie be banned?

ISABELLE: It's the base for studying film grammar. And yes, for problems of representation—

SAFINA: He makes Black people evil.

ISABELLE: I can see that. But remember, look at it critically, objectively, with historical context—

SAFINA: *(from the film)* "The helpless white minority." "Defence of their Aryan birthright . . . "

JORGE: She said historical context.

SAFINA: From 1915. Every movie ever since has editing. Most without blackface. Take your pick.

ISABELLE: Excellent. Ask yourselves: Have we made progress since this film? How does the systemic racism persist?

SAFINA: What if I told the dean you're forcing us to watch this alt-right disinformation.

ISABELLE: . . . Wow. I did suggest alternatives to *The Birth of a Nation*. The school deems this film mandatory. Flawed works still have value to teach us—

SAFINA: And you're leaving up posts on the board, like, you didn't delete when someone said . . . you know, "Negro."

JORGE: About *Birth of a Nation.*

SAFINA: Leaving up weird videos.

JORGE: Safina . . .

ISABELLE: Perhaps your paper could argue against the portrayal of race in *Birth of a Nation.* But first, you'd have to watch the film to make a fair argument.

JORGE: We don't have to just talk about editing and whatever?

ISABELLE: Your papers and projects can be about anything and whatever. I want you to think about film in a bigger context, not just techni— Listen, guys, cinema does not exist in a vacuum. Let's open our minds. Cinema may very well be our mirror to society, or better yet, the hammer that smashes the— Know what I mean? How cinema shapes our ethics and morals, responds to, or causes, events in history, why you think a film should be banned . . .

JORGE: So we can write a paper on, like, when *Birth of a Nation* was released, the riots that broke out, the attacks on Negroes?

SAFINA: Oh my gosh.

JORGE: They were Negroes in the movie.

RICHARD: They were also called worse. Doesn't mean we're allowed to say that in the classroom.

ISABELLE: Everything's "allowed" here, guys—

RICHARD: *(to ISABELLE)* That's a terrible idea.

ISABELLE: . . . if you keep it in context.

SAFINA: What's the context of that video from last week?

JORGE: Leave it up.

ISABELLE: Which video? The Ryan Gosling?

SAFINA: Coffee. What's that all about?

JORGE: About Spike Lee rules?

SAFINA: What's wrong with interracial? My mom and dad are.

JORGE: Then why're you so anti-white if you're half?

SAFINA: I'm three-quarters, but you don't see that, do you?

JORGE: *Jungle Fever* is all *for* interracial.

DAVINDER: But they combined that *Jungle Fever* clip with, like, a quote *against* integration. BTW, I didn't post it.

RICHARD: Me neither.

JORGE: *(about SAFINA)* She did. Chip.

JORGE flicks a chip off her shoulder.

SAFINA punches his arm.

ISABELLE: Okay, *that's* not allowed. Doesn't matter who posted, what matters is what do you think they're trying to say? . . .

ISABELLE gestures to DAVINDER.

DAVINDER: Davinder. I already posted my thoughts and got so totally flamed. "Dirty faggot."

JORGE: I got called that too. I don't think it's personal, Dav.

DAVINDER: *(to ISABELLE)* What do you think they're trying to say with *that*?

ISABELLE: Let's finish our thoughts on *Jungle Fever* first.

DAVINDER: Why is my thing less important? So, like, race over queerness? Excuse me—

Points at themself.

Brown.

ISABELLE: We *will* find time for your concern. This video demonstrates one of our subjects: Soviet montage. Juxtaposition.

DAVINDER: So, like, pretty much intersection? That's pretty much me.

RICHARD: Dav's got a point. The video's converging two parts of equal value to say . . .

SAFINA: . . . Don't mix. Shouldn't *you* be upset?

ISABELLE: No.

SAFINA: Did you even see the clip?

ISABELLE: Yes.

RICHARD: What do you think they're trying to say?

ISABELLE: Maybe the student's showing us how toxic it is when we don't consider opposing views.

SAFINA: Maybe the student's a racist.

JORGE: Maybe the student's working out some guilt.

SAFINA: *(to ISABELLE)* Is *that* allowed? Where's the context in that?

DAVINDER: I think you need to delete some posts.

Bang. ISABELLE slams the door shut. She has come home. LEE is on her laptop.

ISABELLE: These fucking kids make me wanna blow my brains out.

LEE keeps typing.

Everything's *gotcha!* like waiting for me to fail, step on their moral landmines, I'm gonna get a call from the NAACP . . . How are you?

LEE: Ssshhh . . .

ISABELLE: I want what they want, same endgame, but I'm not *righteous* enough, not one-of-them enough . . .

Typing.

. . . I wanna listen to all sides, now I'm not *pure* enough— Let me teach you nuance and you'll see I'm on *your* side!

Typing.

Am I threatening?

LEE: Ha.

Typing.

ISABELLE: Can I show you something?

LEE: I'm writing.

ISABELLE flutters her fingers randomly all over the keyboard. A flash of typing mess. LEE grasps ISABELLE's hands.

Astonished, playful shock on LEE's face.

You cunt!

ISABELLE: Lemme log on to my . . .

She logs on to the discussion board.

LEE: The NAACP?

ISABELLE: Possibly ACLU, PETA, NASA . . .

LEE: Should I be worried for my white girl?

ISABELLE: Always. Look for a video by Richard69.

LEE: *Fine* . . .

STUDENTS at computers. Some spoken lines are also projected.

BruckheimerFan93 says:

STUDENT: *(projected)* "im not sure i get how eisensteins montage relates 2 helegian dialtics"

ISABELLE: He means Hegelian dialectics.

LEE: I know. Here's a reply:

STUDENT: *(projected)* "BF93, its combining oposite ends like asss to mouth, u fag!!!"

LEE: This is atrocious.

ISABELLE: "Fag" is a bit excessive.

LEE: I mean their spelling. Do they write their assignments like this?

ISABELLE: A few less LOLs. You should know.

LEE: I teach writing. Therefore my students can write. Don't film kids take an English prerequisite at your school?

(projected) "when i first saw isabelle i tried to pick her up! i thought she was a student! uh oh!"

ISABELLE sits in the chair with LEE.

STUDENT: "You can't anyway. She's married."

STUDENT: "To a woman."

STUDENTS: *(smattering)* "NICE. / I knew it. / Doesn't look like one. / So what. / Good for her!"

ISABELLE: Shit. I said no gossip.

LEE: There's no gossip on a university-*regulated* board.

ISABELLE: Lee, watch the video. You get groceries yet?

She checks the refrigerator. Only condiments. One apple.

Nope. Ketchup for dinner. Order in?

LEE: "I've read her wife's first novel, from ten years ago. Intense relationship between two rebellious women. *Baise-moi*-esque. Or autobiography? Got me fired up." By Ricki13. How's this kid know about us?

ISABELLE: Because the Internet. Hey, when can I read your new draft? When do you need feedback?

LEE watches the clip from Jungle Fever. *ISABELLE joins her with the apple and a knife.*

Projection: "The only thing I like integrated is my coffee."

What do you think?

ISABELLE cuts slices of apple, eats some, feeds some to LEE.

LEE: Still revising.

ISABELLE: No, the video.

LEE: I like Spike Lee. But . . .

ISABELLE: Does it bother you?

LEE: Depends on this kid's intention.

ISABELLE: What if they don't mean to offend but someone gets offended anyway. They're being misinterpreted, or being—

LEE: A dick. Is this kid mixed?

ISABELLE: What if they were? Gives them permission?

LEE: Gives context.

ISABELLE: Exactly. We don't know the whole story.

LEE: What's your verdict?

ISABELLE: It's worth leaving up for discussion.

LEE: What's to discuss? Black man, white woman, no integration. Is it about you?

ISABELLE shrugs.

ISABELLE: A student called me out for not deleting. Apparently this should upset me.

LEE: Doesn't it?

ISABELLE: Look at the *Jungle Fever* side, no, why would it upset me? It's not addressed to me, not addressed to her. You've met her. My office. Safina.

LEE: I could see her taking this personally.

ISABELLE: She's sensitive. She wants to ban films. She probably burns books.

LEE: Have you thought about how she feels?

ISABELLE: I'm more interested in how she thinks. She said she's also white, by the way.

LEE: But she'll always be treated as Black. Same with our kid, unless you want them to be hundred-percent saltine.

ISABELLE: Fuck no. I want them to look like us.

LEE: Then listen to the girl. Delete.

ISABELLE: No.

LEE: No?

ISABELLE: I can't. It's against policy.

LEE: Whose policy?

ISABELLE: Mine.

LEE: It's okay to change your mind.

ISABELLE: How about I change theirs. Whoever made this probably isn't racist. Look at the stupid bullshit *we* say to each other under this roof.

LEE: This is our home.

LEE points at the screen.

That is out in public. That is out in your work. You can't be integrating your job with our stupid bullshit, forget coffee. You know what this thing makes you look like?

ISABELLE: Lee. Have I *ever* done anything outright racist.

LEE: No. But now doing nothing makes you look complicit.

ISABELLE: I can see how it *could be* offensive, but it's not clear cut. I'm not gonna rob them of this opportunity to be challenged. You're supposed to be cheering me on.

LEE: "Fag" is pretty clear cut. Gonna leave that up too?

ISABELLE: If I delete one thing, that's the precedent, then I'll have to censor everything, even if it's about film.

LEE: Film.

LEE AND STUDENT: "Who's making #sandwiches for craft services?"

LEE AND STUDENT: "i wish isabelle wud teach me her theory of butts."

LEE: "I'd like to do a group project on *The Birth of a Nation*, if anyone's interested."

ISABELLE: Film.

LEE: RomComQueen247. Good apostrophes. There's a reply:

The following reply is a single line split up between STUDENTS.

STUDENT: "I'm intrigued by how the film portrays the mulatto character Silas Lynch . . . "

STUDENT: " . . . who represents how unconventional unions create discord."

STUDENT: "His white blood is tainted with Negro blood . . . "

STUDENT: " . . . and the result is a villainous rapist."

STUDENTS: "Count me in."

LEE: Jesus Christ . . . By Richard69. Please tell me he's a Black kid.

ISABELLE: If it's the kid I'm thinking, he used "Negro" in context.

LEE: What'd you do about it?

ISABELLE: Hello: *Birth of a Nation.*

LEE: Did *you* say it?

ISABELLE: Lee.

LEE: So you won't but they can? Complicity. "Richard69, no way am I gonna work with someone who speaks as ignorantly as you."

ISABELLE: "You ought to recognize, RomComQueen247, that I said '*Negro*' in the context of the film. Be thankful that I didn't say . . . "

LEE: Say what.

Silence.

You gonna leave that up?

ISABELLE remains silent.

ISABELLE in the lecture hall.

The corresponding images from Battleship Potemkin *can be shown when mentioned.*

ISABELLE: Thoughts?

DAVINDER: The lion statues.

ISABELLE: What do they suggest?

DAVINDER: Nothing. Not by themselves, anyway. Like, the shot of the lion sleeping, the shot of the lion getting up . . . they're just, like, fragments. But connect them together they mean . . . Attack.

ISABELLE: Is that what Eisenstein meant?

DAVINDER: I think.

ISABELLE: Exactly. *Think.* The meaning is created up here: *(points to her temple).* Thesis *(holds out fist)*: soldiers pointing rifles . . . plus Antithesis *(holds out other fist)*: peasant woman getting shot . . . equals Synthesis *(points to her temples)*: Massacre. Revolt. Eisenstein's dialectical approach to montage was deliberate, leading you to a specific meaning. Therefore:

STUDENTS: . . . PROPAGANDA!

ISABELLE: Exactly! The Soviet theorists advanced the editing techniques developed by Griffith, taking a highly intellectual . . . Yes.

DAVINDER: But I don't think *Birth of a Nation* was propaganda.

ISABELLE: Please elaborate . . . um . . .

DAVINDER: Davinder. Still getting flamed.

ISABELLE: Davinder.

DAVINDER: The point is, how could Griffith's *editing*, like, start an uprising?

JORGE: Because you're so wrong, that's how. *Birth of a Nation* was propaganda hardcore. The shot of Negroes—

DAVINDER: Dude.

JORGE: Dude.

ISABELLE: Finish your thought.

JORGE: The shot of Negroes—

SAFINA: Jorge.

JORGE: . . . the shot of *Black African Americans* attacking, cut to a shot of White Knights in shining dunce caps riding horseback making Aryan Nations great again—

SAFINA: Can we drop Griffith?

JORGE: I'm not done.

SAFINA: We're talking about *Potemkin.*

JORGE: . . . All I see is KKK saving / the day—

SAFINA: All you see? You're part of the / problem—

JORGE: CAN YOU LET ME SPEAK?

ISABELLE: Do you— Jorge?

JORGE: Jorge.

ISABELLE: Do you think Griffith meant to inspire an uprising against *African Americans*?

JORGE: Hells yeah. Or maybe he was misunderstood—that's debatable.

SAFINA: There's nothing to debate.

ISABELLE: Sure there is. Is a filmmaker responsible—

SAFINA: *Yes.* Debate closed.

Pause.

ISABELLE: . . . For how their film is interpreted in spite of their intentions?

RICHARD: Certainly. Accountability. Otherwise they're like a troll.

SAFINA: *(to JORGE)* Right?

JORGE: I didn't even post in that thread.

ISABELLE: What's up?

SAFINA: Why didn't you delete that thing about *Birth of a Nation*?

RICHARD: Not saying you're responsible for that post, but . . .

DAVINDER: Now will you let us vote for an admin to, like, cleanse everything?

SAFINA: The N word.

ISABELLE: You all had an important discussion about who gets to say what. Many students expressed learning something new and valuable. Even the original poster said that. And apologized.

SAFINA: Cool. The word's still up.

ISABELLE: It was in quotation marks, used rhetorically. To be dissected and criticized. Which you all did.

SAFINA: Will you take it down?

ISABELLE: *(back to lecture)* Eisenstein used montage to—

RICHARD: Why don't you show us *Intolerance*?

ISABELLE: That's . . . a great idea. I'll set up a screening of *Intolerance*, Griffith's response to *The Birth of a Nation*, the controversy. You're all invited, like film club. Fun! Cool?

SAFINA packs up and leaves.

So that's Eisenstein glorifying the Russian Revolution . . .

DAVINDER leaves in solidarity.

. . . Let's look at Leni Riefenstahl glorifying Nazism with *Triumph of the Will* . . .

Bang. ISABELLE slams her office door shut and slumps into her chair. She begrudgingly opens up the discussion board. She scrolls through the posts and stops at a video.

Opening title card: "For Isabelle." A montage of clips of Hitler, the Nazis, the Holocaust, the KKK, white supremacists, and lynchings.

She remains still in stunned silence. Her phone rings.

ISABELLE: . . . Hey.

LEE in her office.

LEE: Hi. I'm done early, want me to pick you up or still meet you at the doctor's?

ISABELLE: Where are you?

LEE: My office. What time will you be done?

ISABELLE emails her.

ISABELLE: Check your email. Click the thing.

LEE: Now? Fine . . .

LEE checks email.

What.

ISABELLE: Watch it.

LEE watches the clip.

Silence.

Lee.

Silence.

You okay?

LEE: Fuck.

ISABELLE: From that kid Richard69. Should I post a response? Should I contact him directly? Who do I talk to? I've got a Richard, a Richie, a Rick . . . Over a hundred kids, no one uses real names, could be a woman or—

LEE: Delete it.

ISABELLE: Maybe he wants to start a discussion.

LEE: He's accusing you of being a—

ISABELLE: On our first class I swore I wouldn't delete.

LEE: On your first class you weren't David Duke.

ISABELLE: Now I am?

LEE heaves a sigh.

I showed them *Triumph of the Will.* He's drawing a parallel between Fascist, what . . . phenomenology, and . . . what do you think? He's speaking metatextually, referencing Griffith with that shot of the KKK and— He's subverting . . . no, attacking . . . what?

LEE: You. Stop thinking.

ISABELLE: I'm not scared of anything I *understand.*

LEE: Understand your duty is to stop this shit, even if your board is . . . fuckin' maverick. *Phenomenology*? God, what if your department head saw this? Tenure *track* means you're on probation. You know how hard it is for a couple to get teaching jobs in the same city? Raising a family? How long's the video been up?

ISABELLE checks the posting.

ISABELLE: Posted half an hour ago.

LEE: Any comments?

ISABELLE: Not yet.

LEE: Good. Delete it before anyone sees it . . .

ISABELLE: Lee . . .

LEE: . . . Before the dean sees it. What?

ISABELLE: He posted during class.

LEE: Christ. He's *making* this shit in front of you.

ISABELLE: But why? . . . Oh fuck. Before I showed them the Nazi film, they were arguing about, giving me shit for his post from last week.

LEE: You didn't delete the N word.

Pause.

ISABELLE: They're having a critical conversation. Would you rather I erase everything and no one learns?

LEE: You're showing *me* things I already know.

ISABELLE: Okay, I'll stop showing you.

LEE: Are you going to delete?

ISABELLE: No.

LEE: You're not offended by him?

ISABELLE: Nothing offends me, Lee.

LEE: Ask me if I'm offended.

ISABELLE in the lecture hall.

SAFINA: Why didn't you delete that KKK video?

ISABELLE: 'Kay, guys, this is way out of hand. Let's return to Bazin's theory on the long take.

SAFINA: You've made your point.

DAVINDER: Yeah, we get it. What if I showed the dean?

ISABELLE: He would appreciate the discussions we're having.

DAVINDER: You've never had a student complain, have you?

ISABELLE: Did you?

DAVINDER shrugs.

SAFINA: Like, would you leave up a porno video too?

ISABELLE: Pornography's not on our syllabus.

SAFINA: Neither is spreading hate.

ISABELLE: EXCUSE ME?

SAFINA: We never asked to have this shoved on us.

RICHARD: It was shoved on you too. "For Isabelle." Don't you feel violated?

ISABELLE: I feel fine.

RICHARD: How about us?

SAFINA: Totally. Why didn't you give us a warning first class that this would be an unsafe space?

JORGE: *(to SAFINA)* You should've assumed that warning when you set foot on this campus, yo. How can we talk to each other if we're not allowed to say anything? You'd learn something if you gave her a chance. I'm glad that KKK's still up 'cause it's real. We talk so intelligently on that board . . . Sometimes. We speak in complete thoughts, not interrupting like in this argue-fest class. If you can't handle the board, you can't handle real life. And real life has porn.

RICHARD laughs.

But seriously. Can't we look at porn critically? It's a huge part of the movie industry, it's got sex-positive feminists and every letter you'd find at pride parades, it's got like way more social impact than any other genre, but we don't talk about it 'cause it's I dunno why not. I'm gonna post some porn on the board so we can discuss the theory of porno *cinema*.

DAVINDER: Dude.

SAFINA: All you wanna do is agitate is why you're losing followers every day.

JORGE: *(embarrassed)* Well . . . so . . . whatever . . .

RICHARD: I'm still following you.

DAVINDER: I prolly forgot to delete you.

JORGE: Well . . . Haters can hate me. Just being honest and saying what's real like Isabelle.

(to SAFINA) You been checking my profiles every day?

ISABELLE: Maybe let's not post porn.

JORGE: *(to ISABELLE)* 'Sup with that?

ISABELLE: It's off-topic is 'sup.

JORGE: So now we have restrictions?

RICHARD: You're making us watch *Baise-moi*. It's practically porn.

JORGE: For reals? Nice. Show us the whole film—have a fair argument.

SAFINA: I didn't take this course to argue about sex.

JORGE: Naw, you took this course 'cause it's required so too bad. What're you so sensitive about? Let your mind speak instead of your emotions, maybe you'll get somewhere.

SAFINA: Let your mind speak instead of your junk, you'll still get nowhere.

JORGE AND STUDENTS: *(at her audacity, with laughter)* OHHH!

DAVINDER: For the win!

ISABELLE: Guys. This is good. Continue it later.

JORGE: Sure. On the board.

SAFINA: I don't wanna use that thing anymore. It just gets me ticked off.

JORGE: If you don't like it don't read it.

SAFINA: How else am I gonna know what's going on?

JORGE: Call me.

STUDENTS: *(at his audacity, with laughter)* OHHH!

DAVINDER: Legit!

ISABELLE: Bazin's theories opposed the manic editing of the montage theorists . . . Yes?

SAFINA: When are teacher evaluations?

> *ISABELLE in her office checking the discussion board. STUDENTS using devices.*

STUDENT: "TAKE THIS DOWN NOW."

STUDENT: "Why? We can talk about it critically here. We can't in class."

STUDENT: "So why is it censored?"

ISABELLE finds the posted video.

Opening title card: "For Isabelle." A montage of clips of censored interracial lesbian porn. Cut into the clips is the title card "I Feel Fine."

STUDENT: "The only thing I like integrated is my porn."

STUDENT: "I don't see no 'chinks' in this. Where's the diversity LOL?"

STUDENT: "I can't believe you just said that, you ignorant ass."

STUDENT: "I put 'chink' in quotation marks. I was being rhetorical."

STUDENT: "Fixed it for you: ch-nk."

STUDENT: "There are no chinks in this video because it's dedicated to her and her 'n----r' wife."

Pause. She makes a phone call.

ISABELLE: . . . Hi, this is Isabelle from the film department at . . . Yes, you helped me make the discussion board . . . Everything's great. No . . . Yeah, I'm logged on . . . You're on? Do you see the user named Richard69? . . . Yes, porn. Yes, KKK. I'd like to block him. Wait! Can you find out who Richard69 is? Locate him? . . . Can you still block him if he's hiding his IP address? . . . I don't know what proxies are. Okay: block. Wait!

Pause.

. . . Fucking hell. Not you . . .

Breath.

Okay: Block.

ISABELLE at home, curled up on the sofa. LEE enters.

LEE: Incredible! Not a single student at office hours—slayed this motherfucking draft!

ISABELLE: Mh.

LEE: May students never visit me again. What's wrong?

ISABELLE: Nothing.

LEE: What happened?

ISABELLE: You don't need to know.

LEE: Why don't *I* need to know?

ISABELLE: I got another post— Never mind.

LEE: Show me.

ISABELLE: You said don't show.

LEE: That Richard69 kid? Actually: No. Mayumi needs these revisions.

LEE walks away.

ISABELLE: 'Kay bye.

LEE: Is it about me?

ISABELLE: I took care of it.

LEE: What'd he say about me?

ISABELLE: I banned him! Can't post anymore. Nothing to show you.

LEE: Serious?

ISABELLE recites what she wrote:

ISABELLE: "What's up, everyone. I've had to block one troublesome and misguided user from this board. Stay on topic." Fair?

LEE: Harsh.

ISABELLE: Lee! I said I wouldn't block.

LEE: Department made you?

ISABELLE: I made me.

LEE: Good for you. Now those kids'll take you seriously.

ISABELLE: Do you?

LEE sits with her.

I've arranged extracurricular screenings but maybe five people show up . . . I busted my ass to get them free memberships to the Film Reference Library—three people have gone . . . I stay up until four preparing lectures and grading *myself*—you see me—'cause I don't have a fucking TA . . . and you know what I get back? "Get Isabelle a muzzle."

LEE: The board? See, that thing's going above and beyond above and beyond.

ISABELLE: I'm making space for their voices. So many fear getting judged in class, never say a word, can't participate. Told to shut up in life. I'm giving them agency to speak.

LEE: Some of them just want to learn about film, not do hot-button life lessons.

ISABELLE: Yeah, well who taught me to bring that combustion into the classroom?

LEE: Okay, learn from my rookie mistakes if you wanna cause a fuss.

ISABELLE: So your rally was a rookie mistake?

LEE: Equal Pay for Professors of Colour: No. Getting arrested: Yes. Letting things get out of control: Big Mistake.

ISABELLE: I'm making more in my first year as prof than you did. Because of your heavy lifting for all of us. That's no mistake. If *you* inspired me and every student in our class to join you, then why can't I?

LEE massages ISABELLE's shoulders.

LEE: You'll learn there are more compelling ways to inspire people. You can't force your students to join your revolution, can't make them *carpe diem* the shit out of everything. Don't be cute—

ISABELLE: Cute?

LEE jolts her with a quick tickle of the ribs.

LEE: . . . by being clever. Breaking rules with your—

ISABELLE: I haven't broken any—

LEE: . . . with your *ideas.* They'll always beat you at breaking rules. And if things get broken, follow the rules to fix 'em. Like last year, *my* school, a student was harassing—

ISABELLE: And you didn't tell me?

LEE: I never got the emails, other profs and students did. Nothing came out of it anyway. You know why? Someone filed a grievance *as per school policy*, end of problem. You want tenure, you play their game. *Conform* to the institution. I learned this quickly and now look at me: Untouchable.

ISABELLE: No wonder your new book feels bougie.

LEE: Thank you. You know what your problem is? You're hardly ten years older than them. Lived with your mom and dad until three years ago, straight into Ph.D., been a student your whole life. Don't expect them to buy into you.

ISABELLE: I'm like a smart big sister or a—

LEE: Friend?

ISABELLE: Yeah.

LEE: Make them call you Doctor.

ISABELLE: You'd give me a stellar evaluation and hire me again next year, wouldn't you?

LEE: Of course. A baby doesn't fund itself.

ISABELLE sighs.

ISABELLE: God.

LEE: Cold feet? We said five years. Plenty of time to get tenure, then we can focus on the kid. Hell, you're so brilliant you could do it in four years if you play the game. Three. No rush.

ISABELLE: Ugh.

LEE: I would if I could.

ISABELLE: What if I gave birth to an asshole?

LEE: *(drolly)* Choose your sperms wisely.

ISABELLE: No matter how much work I put in, how much faith I place in them, our child could still end up being a troll.

LEE: Okay, we'll make sure our kid's not a troublesome or misguided user or whatever.

ISABELLE: You see! I wanna support them the way *I* believe is right—

LEE: You know you're not this kid's only parent, yeah?

ISABELLE: . . . But what if my way is wrong?

LEE: You can do better.

ISABELLE: You think I'm failing.

LEE: There's hope for you.

ISABELLE goes to the computer.

You wanna make space for a voice? We're doing it. How we raise our baby will be the biggest statement we'll make.

ISABELLE: . . . Checking email . . .

LEE: None of this pink versus blue bullshit, Barbie versus Hot Wheels bullshit, we'll help them grow into whomever they are, support their voice—

ISABELLE: You mean give them agency to speak?

LEE: You're not a failure. You're learning.

ISABELLE: Then I feel like a total learner. Email.

LEE: I'm still figuring shit out too, Izzy. I don't have all the answers—no I do but—

She goes to ISABELLE, *who is frozen at the computer, watching a video.*

Opening title card: "For Isabelle." A montage of clips of censored interracial lesbian porn. Cut into the clips is the title card "I Feel Fine."

ISABELLE: This is my personal email.

LEE: Did you give it to this Kasey Kinder? Student?

ISABELLE: I don't teach a Kasey. Richard69 posted this on the board before I blocked him.

Chime.

New email.

LEE: "There are no chinks in this video because it's dedicated to her and her . . . "

LEE walks away.

ISABELLE: You okay?

LEE: Peachy.

ISABELLE: It wasn't sent to you.

LEE: Are you the one being called nigg—

ISABELLE: "For Isabelle." It's dedicated to me.

LEE: And who? Your *other* wife?

ISABELLE: Anything . . . you wanna . . . say to him?

LEE: Don't engage.

ISABELLE: What would you wanna say? I'll say it as me.

LEE puts on her jacket. ISABELLE types and sends the email.

LEE: What'd you say to him?

ISABELLE: "We are not afraid."

LEE: You included me.

ISABELLE's phone chimes. She reads the incoming text message.

Projection: From Blocked Number: "I forgive you, Isabelle."

I'm out.

LEE leaves, leaving ISABELLE to stare at her phone, alone.

Later. Darkness. ISABELLE *reads the discussion board.* STUDENTS *using devices.*

STUDENT: "It shows real sex! I'm not going to class. Find me at the dean's office."

STUDENT: "She's only playing clips."

STUDENT: "She'll play the whole thing, dirty faggot. She ain't got no censor worth shit."

STUDENT: "Nah, she blocked that Richard69 kid. Hypocrite bitch."

ISABELLE *logs off the discussion board. She goes to the shelf, takes a* DVD, *considers it. A chime. She rushes to check her email. New message. She opens it to find another video.*

*Title card "*BLOCKED*" interspersed throughout. Audio of lesbian porn. Pictures of feminist icons Emma Goldman, Simone de Beauvoir, Germaine Greer, bell hooks, Yoko Ono, Ani DiFranco, Gloria Steinem, Virginia Woolf, Candida Royalle, Margaret Atwood, Kimberlé Williams Crenshaw, Kathleen Hanna, Susan Sontag, Alexandria Ocasio-Cortez. The video ends with a picture of Ruth Bader Ginsburg.*

ISABELLE *types:*

ISABELLE: Expecting extra credit?

She sends.

Her phone vibrates. She reads the incoming text message.

Projection: From Blocked Number: "If you play all of Baise-moi *I will ----- you."*

LEE enters, startling ISABELLE. She is groggy and in pyjamas.

LEE: Can you stop?

ISABELLE: Look at this.

LEE: No. What the hell are you doing?

ISABELLE: Donor research.

LEE: I don't think RBG's our guy.

LEE gets a glass of water.

Let's have my brother over for drinks again, see if he's warmer about being Uncle Dad.

ISABELLE's phone vibrates. She reads the incoming text message.

Projection: From Blocked Number: "If you don't play all of Baise-moi *I will ----- you."*

I'll try again for an appointment with the clinic. A Friday?

ISABELLE: Huh? Sure.

LEE approaches ISABELLE, who hides her phone.

LEE: Who the hell you texting?

ISABELLE: Setting my alarm.

LEE: Come to bed.

LEE kisses her and tries to get intimate but ISABELLE resists and pulls away.

You're a dark dark cloud. Start reading my draft yet?

ISABELLE: Oh, no, I've been—

LEE: Occupied. Don't bother. Mayumi wants changes. Ball-breaker. "Not enough teeth."

She notices the DVD *on the desk.*

You're not showing them *Baise-moi* tomorrow, are you?

ISABELLE nods.

All of it?

Pause.

ISABELLE: Yes.

LEE: Trigger warning, okay?

ISABELLE in the lecture hall. She keeps surveying the STUDENTS.

ISABELLE: . . . The two female characters go on a murderous, sex-filled road trip, which . . . Some people were outraged, calling the film sensationalistic pornography and demanding it be censored. In some markets the title was changed to *Rape Me* instead of . . .

SAFINA arrives late. ISABELLE notices.

. . . the literal meaning. Of the title. Some people demanded the film be banned.

Pause.

In Australia this film was banned. Other countries banned it too, like . . . um. Is the graphic violence gratuitous? Give that some thought. But I'm sure you'll agree with me that the intersection of violence, sex, class, gender . . . race . . . helps intensify its feminist commentary. Here is *Baise-moi* . . .

She is about to retreat.

. . . I just wanted to say, to keep the integrity of this film, like keeping the integrity of our class, that attempts to alter this work or silence this work . . . defang it—that's oppression. From a content rating committee or, or an individual person, it's intellectual *terrorism*, and I want you to take the spirit of this film and say "Fuck you"—

STUDENTS: *(at her audacity, with hooting and cheering)* OHHH!

ISABELLE: " . . . We will not be scared into shutting up." Or whatever it is they want. I have no idea. When this happens we need each other to point out . . . *point out* . . . and expose whoever *among us* tries to terrorize us.

Pause.

We could also talk in private. If you have anything you wanna tell me . . . Anything . . . Here's *Baise-moi* . . .

RICHARD: Does that mean you're making us watch the whole thing?

ISABELLE: *(to the class)* What would you do if I did? Anyone?

JORGE: The whole thing.

DAVINDER packs up and leaves.

ISABELLE: Yes, you can leave. Anyone else anticipate a strong reaction?

Silence. She turns off the lights. Darkness.

RICHARD: If you play all of *Baise-moi* I'll commend you.

SAFINA: You said only clips.

ISABELLE: No clips— Who said that?

Lights up. ISABELLE *surveys the* STUDENTS.

The whole thing.

She turns off the lights and leaves as the film begins.

ISABELLE *enters her office. She makes a phone call.*

ISABELLE: . . . Lee, he's there . . . Richard69 or whoever, he spoke up . . . The lights were off. How do I find him now? . . . How'm I supposed to know you're in a meeting? Call me after? . . . Then can you call me after your lecture? . . . Fine! Say hi to Mayumi for me!

She hangs up.

A chime from her computer. She opens a new email message of a video.

ISABELLE *is giving her lecture from minutes ago: " . . . it's intellectual* terrorism, *and I want you to take the spirit of this film and say 'Fuck you'—"*

Stunned silence. She makes a phone call.

Owen, it's Isabelle, I . . . Good. Not good. I'd like to talk to you about a student . . .

ISABELLE *and* LEE *at home.*

LEE: . . . *Texts*?

LEE puts down a basket of dirty laundry.

ISABELLE: Don't worry about it. I talked to Owen today.

LEE: Who's Owen?

ISABELLE: Department head.

LEE: He'll just tell you to file a grievance . . .

ISABELLE: Don't you have rewrites to do?

LEE: . . . which is what *I* can tell you: File a grievance.

ISABELLE: You don't have the authority.

She takes off a sock and tosses it at LEE.

LEE: I know how it works.

ISABELLE: Let Owen handle it.

LEE: I'm tenured!

ISABELLE tosses the other sock at LEE. She checks her email: no new messages.

I mean, Christ. What'd he say?

ISABELLE: He'll look into it.

LEE: That's it?

ISABELLE: What do you think he should've said?

LEE: Gee, I dunno . . . How about: "Whoa, fisting. Not cool," and— Sending you *texts*?

ISABELLE: He didn't want to judge.

LEE: *Judge*? I would've—

ISABELLE: He needs time to—

LEE: . . . gone to the conduct officer—

ISABELLE: . . . consider the materials . . .

LEE: . . . a meeting with Richard69 or Ricki or Kasey or—

ISABELLE: . . . make a fair . . . *investigate*—

LEE: Okay.

ISABELLE: He's looking into it!

LEE: All right!

ISABELLE: He'll— Anyways: How are you?

LEE takes a calming breath. She puts ISABELLE's socks in the basket.

LEE: She forgot this load of laundry. Bathtub tiles are still grimy. Left her a bigger tip to encourage some effort, but nope. Time for a new housekeeper. You wanna call?

ISABELLE: Or we could clean our house ourselves like regular folks.

ISABELLE has drifted back to checking email.

LEE: Clean? You barely sleep or eat, as if . . . Anything *else* new in life?

ISABELLE: Nothing. Last email from him was seven hours and eighteen minutes ago.

LEE: Did you engage? Izzy?

ISABELLE: More than engaged. I'm in it.

LEE: In what?

ISABELLE: The video of me today.

LEE: You?

ISABELLE: Lecturing.

LEE: Why didn't you tell me?

ISABELLE: Good meeting with Mayumi when I called? Did she call you the next Zadie Smith yet?

LEE: Let's go.

ISABELLE: Where?

LEE: Dinner.

ISABELLE: When?

LEE: Now. We're gonna go out, eat some, some what? Sushi, and then—

ISABELLE: We had sushi on—

LEE: Fuckin' *pad Thai*, and then—

ISABELLE: I don't wanna go out.

LEE: Well I'm not gonna watch you skip dinner *again* so you can keep checking your email . . . Jesus! You've made our place the fucking catacombs . . .

LEE pulls open the blinds.

ISABELLE: Okay. Can we do sushi?

LEE: Where's my keys?

A chime. ISABELLE goes to her computer.

Let's go!

LEE huffs and puts away the laundry basket. ISABELLE receives a rapid succession of chimes and new messages from her laptop and phone.

Projection: Film stills of women being terrorized by knives. Interspersed are pictures of Isabelle Huppert, Isabelle Adjani, and Isabella Rossellini. Each image is a separate message—a storm of chimes and pictures.

ISABELLE checks to make sure LEE is away. She types:

ISABELLE: I'LL . . . FIGURE . . . YOU . . . OUT.

She sends and slaps her laptop shut. LEE returns.

Let's go.

ISABELLE grabs keys off the coffee table and tosses them to LEE. They open the door. Stop in mid-step. Pause. ISABELLE crouches down to pick up something. LEE steps out and looks around. ISABELLE turns back into her home, holding up a Swiss Army knife, opened. LEE returns and locks the door.

LEE: Maybe it's the kids up the block.

ISABELLE: They would place it neatly on our doormat, opened?

ISABELLE shuts the blinds. She checks that the door is locked. LEE watches ISABELLE pace with the open knife in her hand. ISABELLE goes to the window and peeks through the blinds like a stakeout. LEE makes a phone call.

LEE: Hi, I'd like to order delivery . . .

ISABELLE: You know what. No.

ISABELLE leads them out.

Fuck. This.

Just as they leave, she flings the knife onto the floor and slams the door behind them.

ISABELLE in her office. OWEN enters.

OWEN: How are you?

ISABELLE: Fine.

OWEN: I can recommend a counsellor.

ISABELLE: I don't need one.

OWEN: No? This must be overwhelming, suffering this blitzkrieg, never faced so much adversity . . .

ISABELLE: Why do you think I've never faced adversity?

OWEN: I'm on your side.

ISABELLE: Awesome.

OWEN: We want you to feel safe. That's why sometimes we have to consider the students' side a bit deeper, appreciate that they're overburdened and under pressure. No matter what support system we provide, pillows, puppy room . . . Better not get a kid pissed off. Gotta kill all grudges ASAP, just in case.

ISABELLE: Uh, thanks?

OWEN: So you banned this "Richard69" from your board.

ISABELLE: Now he's emailing me. *Texting* from a blocked number. He left a—

OWEN: Who is?

ISABELLE: Ricki13, Kasey Kinder, WilhelmWagner . . .

OWEN: But not Richard69?

ISABELLE: Yes. No. Yes but different names.

OWEN: Do we have evidence they're all *him*?

ISABELLE: I have to start with *someone*.

OWEN: Let's start with a someone *after* your ban.

ISABELLE: How do I file a grievance?

OWEN: That could get the student expelled.

ISABELLE: Yes it could.

OWEN: That's severe.

ISABELLE: That's the point.

OWEN: That could piss them off. Let's look at our options. Now, after the ban . . . Do you find this material offensive?

ISABELLE: I'm a professor of critical thinking. Nothing is offensive to me.

OWEN: Then why'd you ban Richard69 from your thing?

ISABELLE: He was offending other students.

OWEN: Since you banned him has he been disturbing other students?

ISABELLE: I . . . don't know. No one's complained since.

OWEN: Your ban worked. But this new problem, whoever it is, when's the last time they emailed you?

ISABELLE: Last night.

OWEN: The slasher pictures?

ISABELLE: With Isabelle Huppert, Isabelle Adjani, Isabella Rossellini. Then I found a—

OWEN: So there's a relation to film?

ISABELLE: Some materials follow the syllabus. *Some.* Vaguely.

OWEN: Gloria Steinem, Margaret Atwood, bell hooks . . .

ISABELLE: . . . for feminist cinema . . .

OWEN: Any commentary we can think of? Something in class?

ISABELLE: If he wants to criticize a lecture he could just say so, but . . . We're not doing *slasher* movies, Spike Lee . . . Some images are random.

OWEN: I think you're to figure out the links between the images. They're speaking in montage.

ISABELLE: Oh my god.

OWEN: OMG indeed. Isabelle, my sons are fifteen. They've been carrying on conversations for months with friends where they send nothing but photos and videos. Shirtless selfies in the bathroom. Michael Jordan crying. That's how they talk. You should know. You've sent a few GIFs here and there, right?

ISABELLE glares.

ISABELLE: He sent that video of me lecturing. He's recording me during class like . . . surveillance.

OWEN: Like a Dictaphone.

ISABELLE: Huh?

OWEN: It's a recorder that's—

ISABELLE: I know what a Dictaphone is.

OWEN: Perhaps they're dyslexic.

ISABELLE: He is not allowed to record me without consent. That's policy.

OWEN: Do you want me to turn this over to the conduct officer? Turn it over to the police? I would. If it got out of hand.

ISABELLE: When is it finally out of hand? When someone gets hurt? When . . . *this*?

She places the Swiss Army knife on her desk.

It was left outside my home.

OWEN: Whose knife is it?

ISABELLE: It's.

Pause.

I'm not sure.

OWEN: Would you like to talk to the police?

ISABELLE: Would they take this seriously?

OWEN: From you, yes. If you're feeling you can't cope, feeling incapable—

ISABELLE: I feel fine.

OWEN: . . . threatened, we could talk to the police.

ISABELLE: That's the thing. He hasn't explicitly threatened me.

He holds up the knife.

OWEN: You're not intimidated by this? You seem it.

ISABELLE: Tell me how.

OWEN: . . . I'm. Here. We're talking about it.

ISABELLE: My feelings aren't why I called you here. Let's talk about what this is rather than what I seem.

OWEN: Maybe it's some kids in your neighbourhood.

ISABELLE: Have you dealt with a formal grievance before?

OWEN: Grievance over whom?

ISABELLE: Richard69—

OWEN: . . . Who you only know as a bunch of megabytes . . .

ISABELLE: I could use your help with that.

OWEN: . . . Who stopped posting after you made him *persona non grata.*

ISABELLE: Is he your nephew or something?

OWEN: Isabelle. I'd advise you to let Richard69 back on your discussion board.

She laughs.

I won't allow his education to suffer due to your renegade *social media.*

ISABELLE: I won't allow him to continue posting *lynchings*—

OWEN: *Birth of a Nation.*

ISABELLE: . . . Nazis . . .

OWEN: *Triumph of the Will.*

ISABELLE: . . . Hate images, violating students with—

OWEN: And you're not?

ISABELLE: I'm not sending porn, explicit *fucking*—

OWEN: What?

ISABELLE: FUCKING.

OWEN: You showed your class *Baise-moi*. Your syllabus said clips.

ISABELLE: I— The film has no meaning in fragments . . .

OWEN: They have a right to not watch a film—

ISABELLE: . . . they need to understand the whole context . . .

OWEN: . . . starring porn actresses having *real* sex!

ISABELLE: . . . a fair debate about feminist cinema . . .

OWEN: You keep pushing your liberal agenda so hard someone will push back!

ISABELLE: My *liberal agenda*?

OWEN: COULDN'T YOU HAVE SHOWN THEM *THELMA & LOUISE*.

Pause.

You're one hell of a prof. After our interview I wanted to cancel the day, give you the position on the spot: bang. I fought for you. Why? *Vision*. How you saw yourself motivating your students, I knew they'd be inspired by you— You're just like them, but with a Ph.D. You're the same generation. But . . . You're from an older school.

He taps his temple.

It no longer fits here. Your belief that anything goes and everything's valid, they would give that up in order to feel safe. And that's valid. Not everything has equal value, some things are just . . . dangerous. So when you show that film and . . . and *you made a chat board? from where?* . . . and your paper stunt, and . . . "*Negro*" . . . now you want someone *expelled.*

Pause.

A student complained about you.

ISABELLE: About what? About why?

OWEN chuckles.

OWEN: You like taking risks. The student wants me to take action.

ISABELLE: I'm being disciplined?

OWEN: Let's say we're working to avoid discipline.

ISABELLE: Female or male or? . . .

OWEN: It's confidential. Please respect the rules.

He takes the knife to fidget.

This student asked about filing a grievance. I told them to reconsider, but it's their right to make it official if you continue to aggravate. You don't want to put yourself through all this red tape, do you? We'd have to consider it when we review you.

She drums her fingers on her desk.

We want you here. But all it takes is a single tweet against you, against *me* . . . You have to stop escalating, latest issues too, whomever it is. Move on from this. You've got my benefit of the doubt, just like Richard has my benefit of the doubt that he's no longer contacting you.

He turns to leave.

I'll check in with you after—

ISABELLE: Wait. Who's no longer contacting me? Richard or Richard69?

OWEN: Neither. Both.

ISABELLE: So *two* people or the same— Richard69 *is* the student named Richard?

OWEN: Isabelle.

ISABELLE: Owen, don't fuck with me.

He smiles concedingly.

OWEN: Release the block. Richard has a right to access all the same learning tools as his classmates. He's a good kid.

ISABELLE: How would you know?

OWEN: I've met him. Dean's List, 3.9 GPA. He's never been a threat, just misunderstood.

ISABELLE: About? . . .

OWEN: He's not your problem.

ISABELLE: ABOUT.

Silence.

OWEN: He was allegedly pestering at another university last year.

ISABELLE: *What.*

OWEN: *Allegedly.* Rumours. No evidence, no charges, didn't get expelled. Simply transferred here.

About the knife:

I don't know whose this is but I'm sure it's not his. He's never been violent and his non-existent record proves it. His only record is 3.9.

ISABELLE: How did you find the right kid?

OWEN: *He* came to *me*. This morning. Wanted to talk. He posted, was misunderstood, you banned him. He stopped. Do we have any evidence that *this* Richard is emailing you *now*, texting you now? It's gotta be a copycat.

ISABELLE: Richard, Richie, or Rick? Last name?

OWEN: You're coping fine! It's subsided.

ISABELLE: Is it Richard who wants to file a grievance against me?

OWEN: I can't say yea or nay. But I'll get this threat dropped if you drop yours. No one gets cancelled.

He goes to the door.

You've got a lecture to give. I'd stop pursuing this. Let the copycat get bored. It's safer this way.

He holds up the knife.

I'll help investigate. It's outside of school but you're entitled to feel safe everywhere.

She holds out her hand.

ISABELLE: Gimme.

He gives the knife.

OWEN: Have a good class.

He leaves. She grabs her materials and rushes to the lecture hall.

ISABELLE in the lecture hall. JORGE is absent.

ISABELLE: *(distracted, nervous pause)* Okay. Um. Third Cinema. This is a Latin American film movement that denounces capitalism, neo-colonialism, and American hegemony—the dominant power exerting its influence over others.

She surveys the lecture hall full of STUDENTS.

Third Cinema rejects both the Hollywood paradigm and the European art film—

(to a STUDENT) Could you stop typing? Third Cinema . . .

She checks her notes.

Third Cinema— Third Cinema revolts against the establishment, fighting the ideology forced upon them, using film as a weapon to . . .

She checks her notes again.

Third Cinema should be exhibited secretly to avoid censorship . . .

And then crumples them.

. . . about entitlement and Angola . . . post-colonial societies subsided over race and GPA . . . Solanas and Getino's manifesto . . . 1972, directed by Sarah Maldoror, here is—

Scrunched paper ball in her hand.

. . . *Sambizanga.*

She pauses to collect herself. She turns off the lights and starts the film.

Is someone texting? No texting, no *recording* . . . Is Richard here?

Silence.

ISABELLE and LEE at home. ISABELLE is curled up on the sofa, tense. LEE is across, away.

LEE: Fuck Owen. But he's right: copycat. Could be anyone now. Just kill that board. Post one explanation: "I am shutting down the discussion board because you are all fucks."

ISABELLE: No. Group projects are in full swing, they're having incredible discussions— They're organizing a letter-writing campaign for diversity in media. I like them, Lee.

LEE: Good! Then stop reading stop blocking stop *policing*. Let your students go all *Lord of the Flies* on the worldwide shithole, so what.

A chime from ISABELLE's computer. ISABELLE perks up.

Did you hear any of what I just said?

ISABELLE: Flies.

ISABELLE goes to her computer.

LEE: If it's the fucktard I don't wanna hear about it.

LEE leaves.

The message is from JORGE.

JORGE: Hey Isabelle. I had an accident last night and couldn't come to class today. I wanted to tell you . . . My group is doing a project on sex in movies and we're gonna make a video installation. You're cool that we're doing more of an art project, right? Jorge :)

ISABELLE: *(typing)* I'd like to review your videos.

She sends.

LEE returns.

LEE: Mayumi wants to meet with the publisher Friday at three. Can we try for the clinic earlier?

Pause.

Hey.

ISABELLE: What.

LEE: Clinic.

A chime. New message.

JORGE: We weren't asking permission. We just wanna give you a heads-up we're doing a video project. Not sure we're down with sending you our stuff.

ISABELLE: *(typing)* The explicit nature could make your classmates uncomfortable. Please send.

Pause. Typing.

I'm not restricting you. Hope your accident wasn't serious. Can I help?

She sends.

LEE: FRIDAY. CLINIC. NOON. ARE YOU AVAILABLE.

A chime. New message. LEE *and* ISABELLE *at a standoff.*

ISABELLE *checks the message.*

JORGE: We *wanna* make peeps uncomfortable, as long as they're thinking. That's the integrity of our class, ain't it? Don't give up! I'll speak up for you if haters gonna hate. I love our class. Things get rough at home when I speak my mind. Maybe I'll send you our videos. Maybe not. We're being critical about the male gaze so it's gonna be dope. Yeah, I was being stupid in the kitchen while making dinner for my little sisters. Didn't hurt too bad. Thanks for offering help. No one ever does that for me. Peace out.

ISABELLE: *(typing)* Jorge. Please send your videos.

She sends.

She turns to LEE*.*

Not for five years.

LEE: You know how hard it can be? We start the process and in some years from now—*years*—we, I dunno, what, we *pray*.

ISABELLE: It can't happen so soon.

LEE: We don't even have a donor yet. You think we're gonna have a Jesus?

ISABELLE: I don't know I'll have a *job* next year.

LEE: It's just a consultation.

ISABELLE: Cancel. I already have a hundred children.

LEE: Who is your priority?

A chime. New message.

ISABELLE: Why do you get to be the one to focus on her work?

LEE: Oh Christ. You are way *beyond* focused. You're a new myopic.

ISABELLE: If I can stop tiptoeing in your writing vacuum, can I tell you the pressure I'm under?

LEE: We're sharing it.

ISABELLE: Are we? Then maybe let's revisit other ways *together*. Instead of *me* giving us this experience under duress.

LEE: Don't you dare say I'm forcing you.

ISABELLE: I have work to do.

LEE: You want this as much as I.

ISABELLE turns to her computer.

And let me tell you, I care about your goddamn tenure more than you do. You go ahead and make, what—*pedagogy* Romantic, fine, I get it. I'll be the one who makes sure your ass doesn't get fired. Not so we can be an academic all-star team, fuck that. So we can build a family . . . Izzy.

ISABELLE is frozen.

Please look at me when—

ISABELLE: Ricki13.

LEE: Who should you be talking to?

LEE goes to the computer to delete the message. ISABELLE impedes. Slight tussle. LEE gives up. ISABELLE hits a key to start a video. LEE walks away, refusing to look at the screen.

A collage. A big photo of ISABELLE's head. Beneath the cut-out of ISABELLE's head are many cut-outs of smaller heads of various Black women (none are LEE). A pair of hands wearing surgical gloves enter the frame, holding a Swiss Army knife. The knife is the one now in ISABELLE's possession.

The hands use the knife to cut out ISABELLE's mouth as a rectangle. The hands peel back the rectangle, revealing on the layer underneath: "HYPOCRISY." The hands cut out her ear, peel back the rectangle, revealing: "SANCTIMONY." The hands cut out her eyes, peel back the rectangle, revealing: "HEGEMONY."

What, more fisting?

LEE joins the transfixed ISABELLE to watch.

Audio of ISABELLE giving the lecture about Third Cinema: ". . . hegemony—the dominant power exerting its influence over others."

Out of frame, one glove is removed. The gloved hand slices the palm of the naked hand with the knife. Blood drips all over ISABELLE*'s mutilated paper face. A close-up on the wounded palm.*

The operation is calm. The sounds from this operation are audible. No sound effects or music.

The video appears to be created by a single person—the camera mounted on a tripod, not held by a camera operator. By using gloves and keeping the naked palm in close-up, the person's sex, skin tone, etc. are not easy to discern. The hands could be from anyone. Anonymous.

Who were you chatting with earlier?

ISABELLE *is frozen.*

ISABELLE: What's he saying—

LEE: Anything he wants. You opened the door for— This is how he says hi to you. You opened the door for me to be called a nigg—

ISABELLE: I blocked him. They called you *that word* because of his posts, so I blocked him.

LEE: We're still getting blood on our faces. You let it continue. Hanging on to your *ethos.*

ISABELLE: I let that go for you.

LEE: For me. That's one burden lifted off the shoulders of the white—

ISABELLE: The white what? You don't get to do that anymore.

LEE: I don't get to do *what*? I'm not allowed to speak? Feels familiar. So does fighting back and not a damn thing changes.

(about Ricki13) Talk to him. You'll learn. I'm out.

LEE turns to leave.

ISABELLE: Running off to meet Mayumi to get spell-checked.

LEE: Publisher's annoyed, Mayumi's doubting my work, I can't write—

ISABELLE: You ask who's *my* priority?

LEE: I keep giving psychotherapy to you *and* me for this sick fuck, I can't be home—

ISABELLE: You think I don't see what you're going through?

LEE: In my own home I can't speak, but he does! He speaks through you.

Pause.

I don't know, do you really want a preciously *mixed* baby or is it just good optics.

ISABELLE: If you're doubting who I am because I'm trying to make sense of an MPEG . . .

LEE: My Izzy isn't this reckless.

ISABELLE: . . . because I'm trying to understand him . . .

LEE: So you can *wake him up* and do *justice*—?

ISABELLE: . . . then you've let him get through to you, unchallenged . . .

LEE: He's not worth my fight. Know what is?

ISABELLE: . . . never learning why he's wrong.

LEE: My accomplishments prove him wrong.

ISABELLE: . . . What is justice to you?

LEE: MY SUCCESS.

ISABELLE: You'd rather break into *New York Times* Best Sellers—

LEE: You can't save him!

ISABELLE: . . . not break through to *him*.

LEE holds up the knife.

LEE: IS YOUR FIGHT WORTH *THIS*?

She storms out the front door.

ISABELLE: Where you going?

LEE: My sister's.

ISABELLE: Don't . . .

ISABELLE stands very alone. She types a reply.

Meet me in my office.

ISABELLE in her office. She sits at her desk staring at the open door anxiously. DAVINDER enters.

ISABELLE: Davinder. Nice to see you. What's up? Have you seen Jorge? How's his hand?

DAVINDER: No idea.

ISABELLE: You can leave the door open.

DAVINDER: I just wanted to say that you're awesome.

ISABELLE: Oh.

DAVINDER: You're super cool and your class is actually kinda fun like *Real Housewives* fun.

ISABELLE: Oh.

DAVINDER: I'll never watch movies the same way again, like, you've given us a new language or something.

ISABELLE: Aw, well, there were times I wasn't sure I was being a good influence.

DAVINDER: Ummm . . . So when teacher evaluations come I gotta be honest and say how awesome a prof you are, 'cause you are.

ISABELLE: Thank you!

DAVINDER: No no. You are. You're good. *But* . . . Like honestly, how could I not mention the board? Like that video—

ISABELLE: Which video?

DAVINDER: Cutting up your face.

ISABELLE: Is on the board?

DAVINDER: What's *not* on the board? Surprised?

ISABELLE: Just felt a bit . . . personal.

DAVINDER: Yup. Like, stings, doesn't it?

Pause.

Are you dealing okay?

ISABELLE: I'm . . .

DAVINDER: . . . Fine? Maybe it's not real.

ISABELLE: Do you know who Ricki13 is?

DAVINDER: That's not the point. That video—

ISABELLE: How well do you know Jorge?

DAVINDER: *I* posted—

ISABELLE: *You* posted?

Pause.

Videos last night?

DAVINDER: Sure.

ISABELLE: What are you saying to me with that video?

DAVINDER: The point isn't the video. I posted *about* the video and I'm getting ripped to shreds like whoa. Over two hundred comments attacking me, other students— Didn't see that, did you?

ISABELLE: Do you have my personal email?

DAVINDER: The point isn't your email. Look at the board. All the attacks on me from day one are still there, except on the posts you deleted when you said you wouldn't delete, when you blocked that guy. If you're gonna moderate on one, why not moderate everyone? They hurt. I dealt with this all through high school and I thought I could leave it all behind when I got to university. And I did. I don't get attacked in any of my courses, just yours. You've, like, brought it all back.

ISABELLE: Let's think of a response that'll work.

DAVINDER: Anything I say makes it worse. But the point is, here's the thing: Make me the moderator. Admin. Whatever. My boyfriend's in IT and he can do this if you don't know how. I'll clean it all up and I won't mention the board in your evaluation because, like, problem solved, right?

ISABELLE: You do this with all your teachers?

DAVINDER: *You* understand what I'm going through.

Pause.

ISABELLE: Let me sit with this.

DAVINDER: Honestly, I wanted to bring this up with Owen for weeks. But I wanted to give you a chance because you're awesome. So . . .

ISABELLE: I'll think about it.

DAVINDER: What is there to think about?

DAVINDER heads to the door.

ISABELLE: Did you file a grievance?

DAVINDER: Not yet.

DAVINDER leaves, shutting the door firmly. ISABELLE stares at the door.

A knock.

ISABELLE: Who is it?

Silence.

WHO IS IT?

SAFINA: Safina from Theory.

ISABELLE: Come in.

She enters. She accidentally slams the door shut.

Could you please open the door? School policy.

She opens the door.

Is anyone else out there? Jorge, not Jorge? . . .

SAFINA: Seeing him soon. Want me to tell him anything?

ISABELLE: No, I'll take care of it. What's up?

SAFINA: I'd like to talk about my paper.

SAFINA sits in a chair by the door. She puts her binder down.

I'm writing about *Baise-moi*. You told us all these layers of oppression—class, gender, race—so the film's totally not just about women overpowering men. Since one of the characters is Arab, I wanna look at minorities overthrowing authority. We didn't talk too much about it in class: Arab versus the French.

ISABELLE: The focus was feminist cinema.

SAFINA: But I see parallels between *Baise-moi* and Third Cinema.

ISABELLE: Excellent!

SAFINA: I'm making a post-colonial argument, about fighting back against Western hegemony.

ISABELLE: . . . You're into hegemony.

SAFINA: Not *into*-into. It offends me. Everything I've read centres around the feminism—

ISABELLE: Offends you enough to do something about it.

SAFINA: I already am.

ISABELLE takes out the knife and places it on her desk, close at hand.

ISABELLE: Do you recognize this knife?

SAFINA: Looks like the one in that video. It's so wrong!

ISABELLE: Show me your hands.

SAFINA: You can't do that.

ISABELLE: Your hands.

SAFINA: It's my body.

SAFINA slides her hands into her pockets. Impasse.

Why would I make it?

ISABELLE: Then who?

SAFINA: Says so right on the board.

ISABELLE: I don't read the board anymore.

SAFINA: Then how'd you see the video?

ISABELLE: You tell me.

SAFINA: I'd rather talk about research.

ISABELLE: Emailed me.

SAFINA: Creepster. Why don't you read the board anymore?

ISABELLE: Trying *Lord of the Flies*.

SAFINA: Huh?

ISABELLE: Just . . . listening to some advice.

SAFINA: I've got advice. Get back on and delete or I'll— I went to the dean's office.

ISABELLE: Dean's office.

SAFINA: This class is so . . . I can't say a single word on the board without getting torn up.

ISABELLE: What if I got your classmate to moderate?

SAFINA: Whoa. You would?

ISABELLE: I'm thinking about it. Would that make you feel less . . . complaint-like?

SAFINA: That's not all I'm feeling. I'm getting panic attacks, but I can't tell my mom or dad it's the Internet again.

ISABELLE: Hm.

Pause.

How do the films make you feel?

SAFINA: I was hundred-percent uncomfortable with your choices . . .

ISABELLE: Everything I've shown was approved.

SAFINA: . . . And then you played all of *Baise-moi*.

ISABELLE: . . . ish.

SAFINA: I can't believe you dared.

ISABELLE: Can we discuss your grievance before you—

SAFINA: Grievance with that film? I wanna make a film like that. A big F-off to racist sexist dude assholes. Sorry.

ISABELLE: No no, this is good.

SAFINA: Something that shocks you into like, "Wake up! This world sucks!"

ISABELLE: It does!

SAFINA: Yeah, so . . . Thanks for showing us. I wasn't even gonna go. I was waiting at the dean's office but just had to go see if you'd play the whole thing. You're pretty brave. I told my mom about you. Good things.

Pause.

ISABELLE: Are your parents still together?

SAFINA: Oh, totally.

Pause.

Am I in trouble?

ISABELLE: No, just . . . Nice to know.

SAFINA: Gotta run. Meeting about the group project.

SAFINA gets up.

So do you have any ideas about research?

ISABELLE: Oh.

SAFINA: It's okay. I can visit again.

ISABELLE: Have you seen Jorge?

SAFINA: Saw him the other night. Seeing him in a minute.

ISABELLE: You're in his group project?

SAFINA: He's in *my* group project. Male gaze.

ISABELLE: You . . . two . . . working together?

SAFINA: I know, right. We're learning. It's . . . dope. He forwarded us your emails. You wanted our videos?

ISABELLE: Were you with him when he hurt himself?

Pause.

SAFINA: Yeah.

Pause.

ISABELLE: . . . Yeah?

SAFINA: He's always hurting himself.

ISABELLE: What does *that* mean?

SAFINA: He's Jorge. He's like a cat. Bye!

She leaves, slamming the door shut.

(off stage) Sorry.

ISABELLE: Cat?

A knock at the door.

Come in.

RICHARD enters.

RICHARD: Hi. Am I disturbing?

ISABELLE: No, office hours.

RICHARD: Great! How are you?

ISABELLE: Oh you know. Theory.

RICHARD: Yes. I've got a concern about my paper.

ISABELLE: What's up? Oh, I'm Isabelle.

RICHARD: I know that!

He shuts the door. He sits in a chair blocking the door.

ISABELLE: Of course, it's just . . . interesting to meet students in person.

RICHARD: I agree.

ISABELLE: What's your name? Could you please open the door?

He does not open the door.

RICHARD: Richard. So. What's up. When digital video first came out, everyone was afraid that too many wannabe filmmakers would sully the craft. But time has proven that digital video hasn't replaced the quality of skilled filmmakers, so initial fears were unfulfilled. But *now* anyone with a phone can make a movie, and who has phones? Everyone, so I'm going to examine new fears.

Silence.

And I'd like to create a short video to illustrate my thesis. Would you approve?

Silence.

RICHARD chuckles.

Don't worry, I'll still write my paper. The video is only supplementary.

Pause.

I don't expect extra credit.

ISABELLE: Your name's Richard?

RICHARD: Hello.

ISABELLE: Anything else?

RICHARD: Dick.

ISABELLE: You want back on the discussion board, is that what you want?

RICHARD: What? I've always been on.

ISABELLE: What names do you use?

RICHARD: More than one name? You can do that?

ISABELLE: What names do you use for email?

RICHARD: Richard.

ISABELLE: That's it?

RICHARD: That's my name.

ISABELLE: You're Richard69 on the board.

RICHARD: Um. No one uses their real names. Why did you block him?

Pause.

Thanks for doing that. You can call me Rick, Rich, Richie . . . I've got an omni-morphic name.

ISABELLE: That's not a word.

RICHARD: I know. It won't show up on my paper. Do you get called Isabella?

ISABELLE: That's not my name.

RICHARD: Bella?

ISABELLE: No.

RICHARD: It means beautiful.

Silence. A knock at the door.

ISABELLE: Come in.

RICHARD gets up. SAFINA enters.

SAFINA: Sorry, I um . . . Oh, there it is.

She picks up her binder.

Sorry . . .

SAFINA is about to leave.

ISABELLE: Stay.

SAFINA: Um.

ISABELLE: We're talking about papers.

SAFINA: Cool.

ISABELLE: You asked me about yours.

SAFINA: Yeah.

ISABELLE: We were discussing Richard's . . .

RICHARD and SAFINA wave to each other.

Safina, what do you think about Richard's— What's yours about?

RICHARD: The consequences of increased democratization of filmmaking.

ISABELLE: Yes. And Safina's is about . . .

SAFINA: *Baise-moi.* I'm in a meeting. Sorry.

RICHARD: It's okay.

SAFINA shuts the door behind her.

SAFINA: *(off stage)* Oh right, open.

She opens the door and leaves. RICHARD gently shuts the door.

RICHARD: *Baise-moi.*

Pause.

So how do you feel about my video?

ISABELLE: If you have something to say to me, say it . . .

RICHARD: Sure!

ISABELLE: Not on video.

RICHARD: I'm still writing my paper.

ISABELLE: Not in writing. You're very articulate so go ahead: speak.

RICHARD: The video would speak for itself but only if you approve.

ISABELLE: What if I did approve? What do you want me to do?

RICHARD: Watch it.

ISABELLE: Then?

RICHARD: Grade it. The paper, I mean.

ISABELLE: Show your video to the class?

RICHARD: No no no . . .

ISABELLE: Show your video to the university?

RICHARD: No no no . . .

ISABELLE: Show the world, make you go viral?

RICHARD: No no no!

ISABELLE: How about I show it to the police, you want attention? Haven't you made enough videos?

RICHARD: I haven't made any videos. That's why I'm asking.

ISABELLE: Bullshit.

RICHARD: Um.

ISABELLE: This isn't your production course—

RICHARD: I know.

ISABELLE: . . . This is *Theory*.

RICHARD: I know! I'm not a filmmaker. I want to *write* about film. I suppose I'm an academic like you. I could write a regular old essay about *Citizen Kane* or *Rashomon*, but since you're so open-minded, I'd like to do something different. My video would illustrate the ideas in my paper—putting theory into practice. I thought you might appreciate that.

ISABELLE: Hm.

RICHARD: But I wouldn't want to show the class and I'd certainly never post a video on the board. They'd call me out as an overachiever or a jerk-off. Sorry, that was inappropriate. I don't have to make a video. Stupid idea, sorry to bother you.

ISABELLE: You got my email from yesterday?

RICHARD: About what?

ISABELLE: Meeting me here.

RICHARD: Was it to the whole class?

ISABELLE: Just you.

RICHARD: Maybe you sent it to the wrong Richard. I checked my email just before I got here, nothing from you. What did you want to meet about?

She holds up the knife.

ISABELLE: Does this look familiar?

RICHARD: Nice knife.

ISABELLE: Tell me about this knife.

RICHARD: Swiss Army, right?

ISABELLE: Who does it belong to?

RICHARD: Some kid?

She slams the knife down on her desk. She forcefully grabs both of his hands and holds them out. She inspects. Thoroughly. Very thoroughly. No cut. She stares at a bewildered RICHARD.

ISABELLE: Make the video.

RICHARD: You'll accept?

ISABELLE: Yes.

RICHARD: Great! I'm looking forward to our final day of class.

ISABELLE: Me more. Why?

RICHARD: Teacher evaluations. Someone's gonna get a glowing one from me.

He leaves, shutting the door gently behind him.

ISABELLE *enters her home, dazed and scattered. She lies down on the floor for a while.*

LEE *enters from the bedroom. She stops when she sees* ISABELLE *on the floor.* ISABELLE *lifts her head and connects with* LEE *for a moment.* LEE *gets ready for a meeting.* ISABELLE, *in her daze, manages to pull herself to standing.*

ISABELLE: How was your brother's?

LEE: My sister's. But my brother was there.

ISABELLE: Did you talk about his sperm?

LEE: Gotta run. Book meeting.

LEE searches around for her keys.

ISABELLE: I think my entire class filed a grievance against me.

LEE: Anything you wanna talk about, maybe got something to say to me?

LEE keeps searching for keys.

ISABELLE: Am I gonna get blackmailed by a student every Wednesday?

LEE digs into her purse, her frustration growing. She slams her purse onto the floor.

ISABELLE pulls keys from LEE's other jacket on the chair. She hands LEE the keys. ISABELLE grasps and fixates on the palm of LEE's outstretched, open hand.

That jacket's falling apart.

LEE: You high?

ISABELLE: No, are you?

Still holding her hand.

How are you?

LEE: I'm all ears.

ISABELLE: Ready for feedback?

LEE: Made dinner for you. Use the toaster oven, not microwave . . . So? . . .

Pause.

Fine, bye.

She is about to leave.

ISABELLE: I spoke to Richard today.

LEE: Shit.

ISABELLE: Unless I spoke to the wrong Jorge. 'Cause I told Ricki to meet me but Richard didn't show up, so I spoke to Richard instead.

LEE: Talk about this when I get back.

ISABELLE: Just an update. I'll stop.

LEE: Mail for you.

LEE hands her the mail.

ISABELLE: Hi, Mayumi.

LEE: You okay?

ISABELLE opens an envelope with the Swiss Army knife and takes out a DVD.

ISABELLE: *The Conversation*!

LEE: Who sent that?

ISABELLE: Don't make Thesaurus wait. I still get old films sent to me. The film gods sent it. Coppola sent it.

She plays the DVD.

Go best-sell yourself. I've got a date with the Swiss Army and Gene Hackman. Walk away!

LEE is almost out the door.

LEE: Already gone.

The DVD is a montage of clips of ISABELLE lecturing throughout the past few months, during numerous classes. Then the video cuts to clips of LEE lecturing during numerous classes one year ago. LEE's hair was different. The entire video is silent.

That was last year.

ISABELLE: Still got your class lists—

LEE: . . . from last year. On it.

LEE looks through files at her desk. ISABELLE grabs her phone.

Who you calling?

ISABELLE: Police.

LEE: Fuck the cops.

ISABELLE is dialing.

ISABELLE: What should we say?

LEE: Listen to me. Don't call the cops.

LEE grasps ISABELLE's hands and phone.

ISABELLE: Forget the cops.

LEE: We got this.

ISABELLE's phone chimes. She reads the incoming text message.

ISABELLE: "Check the board."

ISABELLE opens up the board on her computer.

Richard69.

Anxiety. She struggles, attempting to type.

LEE: You can't be talking to him!

ISABELLE: Not to him . . . to everyone . . . shutting down . . .

She braces herself. Breaking down, she doubles over.

LEE: Isabelle!

Projection: "ATTENTION STUDENTS OF FILM 211: Class will be cancelled for next week. This discussion board will be shut down. —Isabelle."

STUDENTS using devices.

JORGE: Attention students of Film 211.

SAFINA: Class will be cancelled for next week.

DAVINDER: This discussion board will be shut down.

RICHARD: Isabelle.

Two weeks later. ISABELLE *at home, wearing home clothes, convalescent. She sits at her desk writing.* LEE *bustles about, getting ready to leave. She places her keys on* ISABELLE*'s desk and demands attention.* ISABELLE *ignores her, busy.*

LEE: Yo.

ISABELLE: Ssshhh . . .

LEE *tickles* ISABELLE*'s ear with her finger, slowly, gently, irritatingly.*

I'm writing!

LEE *shows off her new jacket.*

LEE: Yeah?

ISABELLE: Better without that tag. Come here.

She leads LEE *to the coffee table and picks up the Swiss Army knife to cut the tag off* LEE*'s jacket.*

LEE: Ugh. How can you hang on to that thing? Souvenir?

ISABELLE: Trophy. Now get outta here and let me write.

She replaces the knife on the coffee table.

LEE: A drink tonight?

ISABELLE: Oooh, a date on a school night?

LEE: Celebrate your triumphant return.

ISABELLE: If I finish my work in time.

She turns back to writing. LEE *grasps* ISABELLE*'s face with both hands.*

LEE: You're a good prof.

ISABELLE: Finished reading your newest draft.

LEE: Feedback.

ISABELLE: You and Mayumi put plenty of teeth in there. Fangs.

LEE: Not my editor who inspired that. Keep talking . . .

ISABELLE: Tonight.

ISABELLE *smiles. Back to writing.*

LEE: Where should we go?

ISABELLE: *You* should go to work and *I* should get back to this lesson.

LEE: This ass is walkin' away.

ISABELLE: Oh, do you have a meeting on Friday?

LEE: Nope.

ISABELLE: I think yeah you do. Me, you, your brother?

LEE *smiles and nods.*

LEE: Yup.

ISABELLE: Lee.

LEE stops at the door.

I will do better.

LEE: Bye, love.

LEE leaves. ISABELLE notices LEE's keys on her desk.

ISABELLE: *(calling)* Your keys.

She is about to rush out to give the keys, but decides to place them back on her desk and return to writing.

The door opens slightly.

(still writing) They're right here.

RICHARD enters. He stands at the door, holding papers in one hand. His other hand is tucked in the pocket of his black trench coat. He watches her writing.

What time do you—

She turns around. Silence.

RICHARD: Hello.

Silence.

How've you been?

Silence.

I hope I'm not disturbing.

Silence.

I wanted to see you last week but class was cancelled, office hours cancelled. Were you sick? Sick of the board, maybe?

He chuckles.

Silence.

We all had questions about our papers, but I suppose you didn't read our posts. Hey, we had a poll! "Is Isabelle a good teacher?" It was meant for you to read.

Silence.

I didn't vote. I never take sides. I mean, why would I? What's the point of fighting others when your own people start fighting themselves? "Isabelle's gone too far" flips to "Isabelle's not far enough." Speak freely becomes you're not allowed to say that. Hypocrites. "Is Isabelle a good teacher?"

She stands.

Who do you think won?

Pause.

We all lost: You killed the board. How're we supposed to learn if you pull the plug when we want to talk?

He shuts the door.

I'd like to give you my essay. I know I'm supposed to give it to you at school, but I'm not allowed on campus. I've been expelled.

ISABELLE: Oh.

He takes a step toward her. She backs away. He places his essay on the coffee table between them and steps back. His hand is still in his trench coat pocket.

RICHARD: *(about taking the essay)* Please.

She cautiously approaches the coffee table. She sees the knife. So does he. She gets the essay and steps back.

Could you please read the title to me?

ISABELLE: "The Blind Terrorist: Counterattacking Hegemony, Hypocrisy, and Sanctimony."

RICHARD: Please grade it if you've got the time. I don't know if it'll count anymore—never been expelled before—but, just in case. I wouldn't want to ruin my record.

ISABELLE: Right.

Pause.

What happened?

RICHARD: Something about unauthorized recordings of lectures or something . . . transferring schools or something . . . It's confusing. Have you heard anything about this?

ISABELLE: No.

RICHARD: You don't know who's accusing me?

He creeps toward her.

ISABELLE: No.

She inches toward the knife between them. She keeps an eye on his hand in the pocket.

RICHARD: Me neither. Anonymous. She won't tell me.

ISABELLE: She?

RICHARD: The conduct officer.

ISABELLE: Right.

RICHARD: I don't want to fight it. Either I leave or she calls the cops. It's confusing.

ISABELLE: Sounds like it.

They are both near the knife.

RICHARD: It's okay. It's time to move on. There are other schools, other teachers.

ISABELLE: Get out.

RICHARD: I want to thank you for our time together.

Simultaneously she grabs the knife and he pulls his hand out of his pocket. She holds out the knife. He holds out a USB key. Standoff.

ISABELLE: What's this?

RICHARD: The supporting video. Please.

She takes it. She approaches him with the knife out, backing him away to the door.

(heartfelt) Take care.

ISABELLE: This ends now.

She thrusts the knife toward him. A warning shot. He barely dodges with a gasp.

RICHARD: Okay.

He leaves. She locks the door. She grabs her phone. She decides against calling. She plugs the USB *into her computer and plays the video.*

RICHARD *is in his bedroom, speaking to a camera. The camera is mounted on a tripod.*

Thank you for being a professor unlike any other. I've had teacher after teacher who inspired nothing inside me, including one professor I presumed was provocative but turned out middle of the road. I gave up on them. But you. You didn't disappoint. I appreciate you challenging me. Your principles transcend definition. You go so far in one direction that you end up on the other side. I can't pin you down! Where are you?

She steps back.

But what conviction! Liberating us with your self-righteous hegemony. Sanctimoniously taking over, like, "Be like me! Be like me! My way is enlightened and fair!" You're so blinded by your beliefs that you don't see your offence. Hypocrite.

She scoffs.

May I offer some advice? Keep fighting. Your values are worth it. But only when welcome. Otherwise, we will fight back harder. Please teach that to your big-statement baby, who, I'm sure, will not be an asshole.

She pauses the video. She looks out the window to see if she is being watched. She searches for surveillance equipment. There is none. She presses play.

Your child will be mindful when others are shouting. So, the next time you hijack a film course to spread your gospel, make sure you're considering the thoughts of others instead of weaponizing your own. Try listening to learn—

He chuckles.

Who taught me that? I . . . Wow.

He considers that for a moment. The camera zooms in slightly. A hint of a camera operator's presence.

. . . I've let you influence me. I'd like to take credit for breaking your morals, but I'll give it to your partner. Trust her. There's hope for you to keep learning. You'll figure it out as a teacher. I can only speak for myself, not for the whole class, but I'm cheering you on to find your voice. Thanks for giving me mine.

Pause.

I hope my project's been avant-garde enough for you.

She takes the essay to read the title.

I suppose I won't have a chance to fill out a teacher evaluation, so please consider this video as my personal show of gratitude. You get an A+. Oh, and despite all our troubles this semester, don't worry about it. I've dropped all grievances. I forgive you, Isabelle.

She pauses the video.

She rips up the essay.

She presses play.

RICHARD: *(to CAMERA OPERATOR)* This isn't gonna work on them anymore. Should we stop?

The camera jostles. The CAMERA OPERATOR enters the frame, seen only waist down. The CAMERA OPERATOR adjusts a desk lamp that is lighting RICHARD's face. One of the CAMERA OPERATOR's hands is wrapped in bandages.

The video ends.

ISABELLE remains still and silent.

The doorknob jiggles. A knock at the door.

Blackout.

End.

Afterword

Esther Jun

The first production of this script was a rollercoaster, as I stated in my original director's notes from the 2018 Tarragon Theatre production,

> From when I first saw the play nine years ago, to workshopping it at the Voaden Prize in Playwriting, to countless workshops with various theatres across this city, *Theory* has grown and expanded with the political zeitgeist. Trying to keep up with that zeitgeist has been an intense and eye-opening expedition. Even in the rehearsal room now, with the ever-shifting climate, new layers of *Theory* are being discovered daily.

At the time, Christine Blasey Ford was reliving her trauma during the hearing for the selection of a US supreme court justice, just as my lead actress was grappling with Isabelle's violent home invasion. My predominantly POC cast were delving into the dark side of racist social media as the "alt-right" were stepping brazenly out of the shadows into the spotlight. My other lead actress playing Lee was meticulously working through a long list of microaggressions that were in the script, some intentional, others not. She graciously helped point them out to myself and Norman. She had been with us for several workshops and her emotional labour is the backbone of the script you have before you now. It was an arduous rehearsal process that required a great deal of care. That is what it is to do theatre nowadays. Hard truths about our society need to be excavated, and in doing so we need to care, not only about the characters we are exploring but also about the actors inhabiting those characters. What are their histories and their stories? How does that inform our work? This is my job as a director, to help guide the actors through difficult emotional terrain so they can present it to an audience night after night safely. In this particular process I learned the valuable lesson that sometimes being uncomfortable is the only way forward. Even as a female POC, I am not exempt from delving deep into my own history to see where my own biases or gaps in knowledge lie. Only then can I truly begin to hear the voices different from mine. Listening must be an active verb and requires a great deal of energy, tenacity, and vulnerability. This is also the very thing that Isabelle learns to engage with in the play. Her privilege allowed her the luxury of not interacting with the trauma of marginalized communities, even that of her own wife's.

Finally, though, times are changing. It only took a global pandemic and the state-sanctioned murder of George Floyd (among countless others) for marginalized groups to have their voices cut through society's cacophonous static of consumerism, narcissism, and apathy. As long as we bravely charge into the mire of identity politics and intersectionality, I feel *Theory* will continue to be relevant. Being an ally is hard work—let's roll up our sleeves and get uncomfortable.

Esther Jun originally trained as an actor in NYC and completed her directing degree at Drama Centre London in 2006. She has directed shows across Canada and currently is Artistic Associate at the Stratford Festival. From 2016–18 she was Assistant Artistic Director at Tarragon Theatre. Esther was part of the 2020 and 2016 Michael Langham Workshop for Classical Direction at the Stratford Festival and was the 2015 Neil Munro Intern Director at the Shaw Festival. She also co-created and is Co-Artistic Director of Directors Lab North, the Canadian offshoot of the Lincoln Center's Directors Lab (www.directorslabnorth.com).

Acknowledgements

Sincere gratitude to Sascha Cole, Audrey Dwyer, Joanna Falck, Annie Gibson, Musa Gurnis, Andrea Harris Smith, Esther Jun, Jessica Lewis, Suzette McCanny, Victoria Murray Baatin, Richard Rose, Ari Roth, Serge Seiden, April Sizemore-Barber, Blake Sproule, Andrea Vagianos, Joanne Williams, and Shirley Barrie. And to the many artists from workshops, readings, and performances.

Sincere appreciation to Daniela Atiencia, Vincent Chan, Kathy Moretton, and my friends for being there for me. Represent.

Norman Yeung is a writer, actor, and visual artist. His play *Theory* won the Voaden Prize and was nominated for the Carol Bolt Award. *Pu-Erh* received four Dora Mavor Moore Award nominations, including Outstanding New Play, and was a finalist for the Voaden Prize. Other plays and performance pieces include *The Zoonotic Story* (Stratford Festival/National Arts Centre), *I Know I'm Supposed to Love You* (Touchstone Theatre), *Deirdre Dear* (LaBute New Theater Festival, St. Louis), *In this moment.* (Scotiabank Nuit Blanche), and *Black Blood* (Tapestry New Opera Showcase, with composer Christiaan Venter). *Theory* and *Ms. Desjardins* were recorded as radio drama podcasts for *PlayME* from CBC Podcasts. Norman was a playwright in residence at Outside the March, and has been a member of playwright/creator units at the Stratford Festival, Tarragon Theatre, fu-GEN Theatre Company, Tapestry Opera, and Canadian Stage. As an actor he has worked with the Stratford Festival, the Royal Manitoba Theatre Centre, Canadian Stage, Theatre Calgary, the Citadel Theatre, Thousand Islands Playhouse, LA Opera, Theatre Conspiracy, Vancouver Asian Canadian Theatre, Firehall Arts Centre, Gateway Theatre, and many more. Among his many roles in film and TV, favourites include *Resident Evil: Afterlife* and *Todd and the Book of Pure Evil.* He holds an Honours B.F.A. in Film from Ryerson University and a B.F.A. in Acting/Theatre from the University of British Columbia. Norman was born in Guangzhou and divides his time between Los Angeles, Toronto, and his hometown of East Vancouver, on the traditional and unceded territory of the Coast Salish peoples.

First edition: February 2021
Printed and bound in Canada by Imprimerie Gauvin, Gatineau

Cover design by David Gee
Author photo © Matt Kallish

PLAYWRIGHTS
CANADA PRESS
202-269 Richmond St. W.
Toronto, ON
M5V 1X1

416.703.0013
info@playwrightscanada.com
www.playwrightscanada.com
@playcanpress

MIX
Paper from
responsible sources
FSC® C100212